What Others Are Saying

"Men Love Confident Women' is a MUST READ for every woman that attends my Millionaire Matchmaker events. Adam teaches them everything they need to know about confidently meeting men."

Patti Stanger, The Millionaire Matchmaker

"Women need to realize that men are attracted to confident women. It's just a matter of how you present yourself. Adam's book teaches this concept exceptionally well - I couldn't recommend it more highly"

Barbara Corcoran, Investor on NBC's Hit Show "Shark Tank"

D1292163

"Adam's new book puts the world of dating and relationships into perspective. He breaks down the ideas of "rules" and replaces them with the importance of critical mindsets that we can take with us into every interaction. I will be encouraging everyone I know to get a copy of this book - we can all learn from it."

James Michael Sama, JamesMSama.com, Dating and Relationship Writer (Over 26 Million Readers)

"As the founder of a social networking company, I see women flirt with men all the time. If you're a woman who isn't readily finding success in love, don't get a cat and give up, just read LoDolce's book. It's a game changer if you're open to self-evaluation."

Jennifer Brooke, Co-Founder of TheGoodOnes.co

"LoDolce is refreshing and relatable. This is an amazing resource for ANY single woman who's looking to succeed in the dating world.

Susan Baxter, Owner of HireAWingWoman.com

MEN LOVE
CONFIDENT WOMEN

Thirty-two Confident Female
Mindsets That Drive Men
Wild

Adam LoDolce

This book is dedicated to the hundreds of thousands of Sexy Confidence fans who inspire me every day to follow my passion. This book is for you.

xoxo

Inside you'll find...

32 Confident Female Mindsets

Wait, You Do *WHAT* For a Living?

L ife has gotten super-duper weird over the past six years, let me tell yah.

I'm sitting in my local coffee shop in the North End of Boston and I wish I could just sit down with the "Young Adam" that existed six years ago for a little conversation.

Because that would be an interesting conversation...

I'd happily tell him that he's no longer a management consultant wearing a suit every day to work.

He's no longer forty pounds overweight.

He's no longer terrified of talking to women and desperately trying to find a date.

He no longer questions every word he says, or every move he makes.

Oh, and one more thing, I'd tell him that I now dedicate my life to helping women build sexy confidence to attract the right man into their lives.

Honestly, I have no idea how the "Young Adam" would respond — because he's so distant from the "Adam" that exists today. But assuming he's like most people I meet, he'd probably just say, "WTF? How the living heck did that happen?"

The simple reason is that I learned how to systematically build confidence.

ADAM IN 2008

The slightly more complicated answer requires more of an explanation.

Let me tell you the story of how it all got started.

Flash back six years.

I woke up hung over on a Saturday morning, opened my eyes and wondered, "What the Be-Jesus happened last night?"

I instantly ran to the bathroom and chugged two glasses of water to bring back any feeling of normalcy.

Then the hangxiety kicks in.

Hangxiety, noun: The overwhelming sense of hangover-anxiety you get when you drink too much and know you did something stupid the night before...but can't quite recall what took place.

I looked at my phone to see if I made any bad texting decisions.

Nope — no bad texts.

But then again, I didn't really HAVE anyone to even text.

And then it hit me. BAM!

I haven't met even one eligible female in the past three months of being single.

I thought to myself, "Dude, I seriously suck at dating."

Why would any girl even like me?

I was a total effing mess.

I didn't feel attractive to women, and that's probably based on the reality that no girl had been attracted to me in quite a while.

I had hit dating rock bottom (dating rock bottom usually comes hand in hand with hangxiety).

So there I sat in an empty bed with a pounding headache and a half-eaten bag of Cheetos next to me from the night before.

I was the stereotypical single and lonely guy on a Saturday morning.

This would've been the Adam from six years ago I'd sit across from.

And this was the moment I realized that I needed to figure this stuff out (just like you probably realized it when you bought this book).

I had no confidence and I knew that if this didn't change quickly I'd end up marrying the first woman who came my way...and we know how that story ends (there's a 50% chance of it happening to any of us and it begins with a capital D).

So I did what you probably did when you found SexyConfidence.com. I hit the internet and started searching for answers.

I bought all of the informational products/books/DVDs out there. I sadly found out that most of the advice was given by people who didn't understand the current dating scene or were just trying to steal my money by promising me the "perfect girlfriend" in a shocking ten days.

It was all a scam.

So instead of continuing to read the same old "just make fun of her to get her to like you" advice, I decided to face my fears and start meeting people in different ways than I'd tried before.

I started being more honest and upfront about my intentions with women when I would approach them.

I started improving my body language to communicate "playfulness" more effectively.

I started working on myself and discovering my own identity. I developed unique passions, interests and charisma and I learned how to communicate those to people when I met them.

I would try going to different venues, events, parties and would talk to ANYONE who'd be willing to interact with me.

I set social goals to hold myself accountable (just like I do with my own clients).

I'd get rejected…a lot. At first it sucked, then I learned to laugh it off for the hysterical life moment it truly was.

This took some serious effort and dedication, but after six months of aggressively dedicating myself to building social confidence, I got pretty good at it (if I may say so myself ☺).

Now, I know what you're thinking…

I'm just some "horn dog" guy who's going out there trying to pick up girls to get laid.

Well, I'd be lying to you, of course, if I told you I wasn't trying to have sex — because of course I was. I love sex and so do you — and that's perfectly OK so long as you're upfront about your intentions.

But more importantly, I wanted to learn how to really connect with women (and people for that matter) to build great relationships in my life.

I wanted to develop the sense of self that would always remind me that I truly deserve to be with someone incredible.

And within one year, I had been reborn.

But of course, the plot thickens.

Something really crazy starting happening to me. Random guys started asking me to help them go through the same transformation I was enjoying.

I happily agreed.

But before long — these guys were getting such crazy results that people told me I should start charging for "nights out" with me (No, I'm not a male *gigolo*, just a dating coach).

So I started charging a few guys. Then a few more guys would come out — then before I knew it I was raising my rates and it turned into a full-blown business.

And within a few more months, I was able to quickly make the decision: work for corporate world or pursue my new found passion?

The old Adam would've taken the safe route and stayed in the cube.

The new Adam believes in himself and his ability to do anything he sets his mind to (and so will you).

So I quit my job and then things started to get REALLY interesting.

I quickly developed some strategies that would help men approach YOU without being a total creeper (you can thank me later).

It was focused on two core principles: honesty and confidence.

Not cheesy pick up lines — or memorizing weird fake stories to impress a woman — because I learned quickly that women see right through that stuff.

Not just trying to get laid — but building a real emotionally charged connection with women when you meet them.

Not getting blackout wasted at clubs to meet people — but meeting people in more organic environments such as the park or the grocery store.

Women loved it because men were being more genuine.

Men loved it because they were gaining REAL confidence by bringing out their true personalities.

The media loved it because I was young and my coaching was producing hundreds of success stories. I was quickly featured in thousands of media outlets all around the world like MTV MADE (As a MADE Coach), *Men's Health*, ABC, FOX, *The New Yorker*,

ADAM AND HIS MTV MADE CLIENT, RANDALL

Huffington Post — you name it, I have probably been featured in it.

Even the top universities in the country heard about my success stories and started hiring me to lecture to their students about dating confidence. As of today I've spoken at over one hundred of the top universities in the country such as Notre Dame, University of Alabama, and University of Texas.

ADAM HAS LECTURED AT OVER 100 OF THE TOP UNIVERSITIES

It was crazy! It all started because I faced my fears and took tangible action to improve my own dating life.

I learned that confidence in one area of life breeds it in other areas as well. Eleanor Roosevelt explained this concept more eloquently, "You gain strength, courage and confidence by every experience in which you really stop to look fear in the face. You are able to say to yourself, 'I have lived through this horror. I can take the next thing that comes along.' You must do the thing you think you cannot do."

But then about three years ago I was totally blindsided by a new epiphany that was almost as powerful as my hangxiety-induced epiphany three years prior.

Biggest life epiphany to date: *Women need to learn EVERYTHING I've learned over the years of working with men.*

Let me explain how this came about.

I launched a video for men that went viral.

It taught men how to meet women during the daytime (such as at a park or a grocery store) and was featured in dozens of magazines and major news outlets such as *Glamour*, *Cosmo* and CNN.com.

This was the first time women had really seen my stuff — and the response was overwhelming.

Hundreds of women were applauding my efforts and asking me to answer their questions about men.

My initial reaction was to just ignore the questions (because I had never coached women before), but then I started looking a little closer and realized I had very specific and tangible answers to all of their questions.

"Adam, why do men pursue women and then just suddenly disappear?"

Or, "Adam, why aren't more guys approaching me?"

Or, "Adam, how can I connect with a man emotionally instead of just making it physical?"

Or my favorite, "How do I turn a casual relationship into something more serious?"

I was totally blown away!

I wasn't surprised by the questions they were asking, but instead by my ability to immediately know the answer to them.

I had spent so much time meeting so many women in my own life as well as working with hundreds of men on flirtation, confidence and dating — that I unexpectedly became a dating expert for women.

It was a weird thought.

The Adam version of Dr. Phil gave me the chills — ugh.

So, as usual, I wanted to do my research.

I started checking out the other dating advice for women out there and I was not only getting more chills, but I was also getting sick to my stomach.

It was HORRIBLE.

The majority of the advice from other so-called "professional" dating coaches usually fell into one of the following categories:

- ✓ **"Lovey Dovey" Dating Experts** who were only trying to make women "feel good" about themselves by hiding the truth about men. This was doing women a disservice and wasn't helping anyone.
- ✓ **The Painfully Harsh Truth Dating Experts** delivering harsh "rule-based" dating advice that was only applicable in specific situations and made women feel horrible about themselves.
- ✓ **The Married or Totally Disconnected Dating Experts** who haven't been single in fifteen years and have no idea how much dating has changed.

And it was all wrong.

After years of being a dating coach, it hit me that men weren't the only ones who needed help.

Women also needed to believe in themselves and in the value they provide to a man in a relationship.

They needed raw, unfiltered advice from the male perspective to make them FEEL more confident as they were getting out there.

Because knowledge is the quickest way to build confidence.

If you KNOW what to do, then you'll feel confident doing it.

But I struggled with using the word "confidence" for women.

Because women didn't need to be "confident" in the traditional sense of the term. It just felt too masculine.

No, I wanted to think of exactly what I would describe to be the perfect woman.

Then it hit me.

Sexy Confidence.

A feminine, confident woman.

When I thought of Sexy Confidence, I thought of the woman who doesn't wait for prince charming to just find her, she gets out there and finds him with class and grace.

I thought of the woman who isn't ashamed to want a relationship, but who also loves being single. She's happy regardless, but knows that relationships create a sense of life fulfillment that's unavailable elsewhere.

I thought of the woman who's a dominant force in the workplace, but can come home to a man and relinquish some of the control so he can be the dominant man she so deeply desires.

This book is designed to give you the mentalities of the Sexy Confident women I've met over the years and to avoid the behaviors of the insecure women who question their every decision.

These principles have been vetted by men, and they have been massively success for thousands of women all across the world.

And now, it's time for you to be my next success story. Are you ready?

Why Men Love Confident Women

I t's pretty well accepted that confidence is an attractive quality in a man.

And given the choice between a physically attractive guy with zero confidence versus a less attractive guy with confidence, most women would take the confident guy any day.

Unfortunately, society's impression of what men want in a woman is, I'd say, slightly different.

Ask a guy what he wants, and you might get, "Boobs...," "Butt...," or both.

So what happens? As a society we just assume that men are these simple creatures who only go for physical looks.

We've all heard it before — attraction for men is more "visual," whereas attraction for women is more emotional.

Women like confident men.

And men like hot women.

Simple and easy right?

WRONG.

Very, very wrong.

Now, a confident man might try to date a physically attractive woman just for her looks, but if she's not also self-confident, he'll very quickly lose interest.

The relationship will soon be a mismatch.

Confident guys who are looking for a long-term relationship will also look at a woman's confidence level as being the #1 critical component for long-term compatibility.

Because if he's secure about who he is, he's going to want to share his life with a woman who feels the same way about herself.

Whereas if you think about it, insecure guys will forever JUST be going for beautiful women for one reason: *validation*.

They believe if they finally date an attractive woman, it will prove to the world that they are valuable.

Now for those of you skeptics who say men don't love confident women, maybe your perception of what confidence means is a little off.

Confidence simply means that you are self-assured in your own ability and self-worth. And in dating terms, confidence means that you believe wholeheartedly that you're an attractive, high-value woman. Basically, that you're a GREAT catch.

Because if you think you're a catch, it's going to shine through in every interaction you have with men. And they will definitely pick up on it.

But I think some people say that men don't like confident women because they don't really understand what it means to be a sexy, confident woman.

So let me set the record straight here.

You can be confident without being dominant.

Sure, maybe you're the CEO of a major company and are dominant in the workplace, but when it comes to dating, allow a man to be a man. Have the confidence to take a step back and let him lead and take charge. Assuming, that is, that you like men who can take charge and be dominant.

I know it can be hard, but in order to have the ying, you must have the yang. The only other option is to date a beta male who is probably going to bore the heck out of you, and then you can be the yang, and he can be the ying…

Your choice.

You can be confident AND be vulnerable.

There are a lot of strong, successful, independent women out there who find it very difficult to open up to a man. Remember, it takes confidence to share some of your insecurities and "weaknesses." Only the most courageous and confident women are able to connect with a guy on an emotional level because they understand that connection is created through vulnerability. Don't feel as if you need to always display strength and independence. Even confident people have insecurities. The difference is that confident people aren't afraid to express them (when the moment is right) whereas insecure people try to hide them, or worse, overcompensate for them.

And lastly, but most importantly…

You can be confident without being *masculine*.

Allowing your feminine presence to shine through requires the same amount of confidence as it takes a man to display his masculinity. Speak slowly, maintain a feminine voice tonality, wear a cute dress, softly touch him on the arm as you stare deeply into his eyes. Men deeply desire this feminine presence from a confident woman. This is what creates a beautiful synergy between the two genders.

And if you're still thinking to yourself, "Adam, I'll never be a confident person," just remember, becoming more confident is an ongoing process that requires work every single day. Moreover, even the most confident people lose their confidence sometimes. The only difference is that they put forth the effort every single day to bring it back by continual self-improvement and self-love.

Learn as much as you can by reading books like this, and get out there and practice it. You might have some days when you feel great, and you might have some days when you feel down — but never, never let a man (or woman) tell you that confidence isn't sexy.

And if they do, just realize that it's probably their own insecurities talking. They're overcompensating.

Insecure people are threatened by confident people.

So if you want to attract a confident man, now is the time to project that sexy confidence.

Just Give Me Six Weeks and I'll Mold You into My Next Success Story!

As my gift to you for purchasing this book, I'd like to offer you access to my advanced six week video training program: The Emotional Attraction Formula at an 80% discount. There are limited discounted copies available, so claim your seat today.

*Simply visit **www.SexyConfidence.com/discount80***

MINDSET 1

A Sexy Confident Woman is Happy When She's Single. Relationship Status ≠ Happiness

A s a professional in the "self-help" industry, I've grown to adopt the philosophy of change, improvement and pushing myself to new heights to make myself better.

Now, that's all well and good, right? And I certainly believe in goal setting, in setting intentions, and setting a direction for your life because we all have things we could improve on. Maybe you want to hit your sales numbers, lose a little bit of weight, or even find the next love of your life.

But I've realized something very recently about self-help and the pursuit of constant life improvement that has started to bother me.

And that is — a lot of people set goals based on the premise that who they are NOW is not good enough to be happy.

Let me ask you question. What is actually stopping you from being the happiest woman alive...right now? What is it really?

It's one thing. There is ONLY one thing stopping you right now.

Your expectations.

You expect that once you make $100,000 a year, you'll finally be able to travel and buy the condo, and then you'll be happy.

You expect that once you lose ten pounds, the man of your dreams will suddenly want you.

You expect that if you get a boyfriend, or married, then all of your other problems will suddenly vanish.

Bear with me, but what if the person you are now, reading this book at this very moment, is capable of the purest form of happiness in this instant.

I'm a dating coach, and finding love is fantastic and beautiful, but you need to be happy and content with your life NOW, not later, in order to really attract a great guy.

I need you to remain mindful that nothing that's happened in the past and nothing that will happen in the future really matters more than what's happening in the present. The grass is always greener, so don't forget to find happiness in your life right now by showing gratitude for what you already have.

Just realize that at this moment, you are already happy, interesting, passionate, and successful. If you're not, you might want to take a second look at your expectations of what you THINK will make you happy.

This is not to deter you from setting relationship goals, but instead is really just a reminder that happiness comes from the journey of self-improvement, not from any sort of arrival.

There is no arrival in life. And self-acceptance is just as important as self-improvement.

And most importantly, if you're not happy while you're dating and meeting people, no man is going to want to be a part of your life.

So I urge you to learn, grow and achieve your highest set of goals, but also to find some happiness in the little things. Live in the present, and soon enough you will attract a happy great guy into your life.

Sexy Confidence Success Story

"Adam I just want to thank you for all of your guidance over the past few months. I used to hate being single because I always thought that relationships were the only thing to make me happy. But then I followed your course and developed my own identity — and as you predicted in the course, that was the moment when I got into a GREAT relationship. All thanks to you — you changed my life."

-Melissa, 28 Alabama

To learn how to create a lifestyle that magnetically attracts men, visit sexyconfidence.com/discount80.

MINDSET 2

A Sexy Confident Woman Doesn't "Try Hard" To Impress a Guy. She Always Assumes Attraction and Acts Accordingly.

Confidence is sexy, but "trying hard" is annoying. Just like it's annoying when guys are being cocky pricks around you, I've noticed a lot of women play the same game as well...and especially when they're talking to a guy they really like.

Have you ever gone out at night, met a ton of guys you didn't like, and noticed that they're chasing you around the room? Then finally, when you run into a guy who has just the right vibe, haircut, swagger — or whatever — he instantly flips your world upside down. You begin to question everything. Whether he'd even like a girl like you, why he's even talking to you, or wondering if he's just talking to you to get to your friend.

Then, because you're totally unsure of your "holy worthiness" of this guy, you want to create an instant facade of confidence to prove to him that you're worthy...no, screw that, you want to show him that you're better than him!

Well let me tell yah, there's nothing more frustrating for a guy than when he's chatting up a girl he likes and she's clearly acting a certain way to impress him. It's obvious and totally ineffective.

Well, here are the four ways I've found women play "try hard" and end up losing the guy.

1. Overly Teasing: Now, I do want you to lightly and playfully tease a guy to pique his interest, but don't be mean to the dude and definitely don't kill his confidence. For example, let's say you're at a fancy lounge and you're talking to a guy who's clearly underdressed. A confidence killing meany would say, "You're only wearing a t-shirt, you look terrible." He's going to avoid you like the plague. However, If you want to flirtatiously tease him you could say, "You've got balls wearing a t-shirt here? What is it, laundry day?" delivering it with a smile. If you're going to tease, at least make it a joke.

2. Bragging about Yourself: You wouldn't be bragging about your new Range Rover to the geeky guy in the corner who approached you, so why would you do it with the attractive, confident dude you're now chatting it up with. Don't brag about how great you are, no one cares and he'll see right through it.

3. **Criticizing Others:** A lot of women will go into competition mode with other women and even talk smack about the girls they are with. Or she might start judging other guys at the venue. Don't be Judge Judy. It's insincere.

4. **Rudeness**: Whether you interrupt him or abruptly start talking to another guy right in front of him. These games might work on some guys, but in the long haul it's going to only attract the socially inept guys who can't see what you're doing. Most guys will just be offended.

The #1 way to overcome these habits is by having what I call an "abundance mentality." This mentality basically sounds like this, "If he doesn't try to pursue me, there are a ton of other incredible eligible guys out there who would DIE to be with me." Keep reminding yourself of this reality. And if it's not a reality — make it a reality.

Continue to put the right type of effort into finding the right type of guys in the right types of venues who WOULD love to be with you.

At www.sexyconfidence.com/discount80 I'll give you seven examples of things to say to a guy to playfully tease him.

MINDSET 3

A Sexy Confident Woman Displays a Positive Vibe and Upbeat Body Language

I must say, I'm not the greatest guitar player this world has ever seen, but I can look impressive when I need to. And most people don't know all I did was learn a few basic chords from YouTube.

Now for those a little musically challenged, a chord is a group of notes, and on the guitar, there are some really basic, easy chords to learn. And interestingly enough, you don't need to know that many chords to be able to play a ton of really awesome songs.

There's actually a great video by a band called Axis of Awesome that went viral on YouTube. They play over forty of today's most popular songs using the same four chords.

Now, I'd like you to imagine that when you're communicating — your words are like a guitar chord, and your body language is your rhythm, tempo and speed.

Just like in music, you can be playing the SAME exact chords but they'll create a radically different song. For example, the D, C, and E chords are used for literally hundreds of the most popular songs.

What matters more than the notes you're playing is the rhythm you're playing them.

The same goes with verbal communication. You could say, "My night's been interesting," and depending on how you say it, it could be interpreted wildly differently.

Say it with a smile, and it's a positive.

Say it with a smirk, and it's mysterious.

Say it with a frown, and it's negative.

Essentially, it doesn't matter WHAT you are saying, it matters HOW you are saying it. Your delivery is everything.

Now body language is comprised of two key elements. The first is physical body language, like smiling, touching, hand gestures, body positioning, and eye contact. The second is the fluctuation in voice — or voice tonality.

Focus less of your energy on the words that are coming out of your mouth, and more of your energy on what your mouth actually looks like (are you smiling or frowning).

Learn the four-part system to perfect body language anytime you meet a guy at www.sexyconfidence.com/discount80

MINDSET 4

A Sexy Confident Woman Is Totally Open and Willing to Meet a Man Online. Because Seriously, Why Not?

I'm about to get super nerdy on you, but bear with me here.

Diffusion is a process by which a new product or idea is accepted by the market. A sociologist named Everett Rogers created a simple theory. There are five types of product adopters: Innovators, Early Adopters, Early Majority, Late Majority, and the laggards (these are the final people to adopt a new product or idea).

Laggards are people who don't have an iPhone yet.

Or the people who refuse to buy a kindle.

Or those who have never even heard of Uber or Lyft car sharing services.

Personally, I used to hate online dating. Historically I would focus my coaching programs on helping people meet one another offline because back then, the only people who were online were the innovators and maybe the early adopters — and at the time it was still just easier and more effective to meet higher quality people offline than online.

Now I believe online dating has hit its tipping point, in part, I believe, due to super simple apps like Tinder making online dating easy and quick to sign up. Now I'm finding really attractive, interesting, confident people, who you may not otherwise meet in the real world, are accessible online at the click of the button.

Basically I'm telling you that if you are single and looking and NOT online, you are a laggard. You are a dating laggard.

You don't want to be a laggard.

Don't be that gal and don't fight the future. It has arrived, and it's a great way to just get yourself out there again.

So go ahead, create a profile, start off with free ones on OKcupid or even Tinder if you just want to get a feel for it. Then you can upgrade to Match or eHarmony.

Once you get started, abide by these three core principles to successful online dating:

1. **Create a Positive Profile:** Once you write your profile, do what I call the negativity scan. If there's a single statement in your profile that could be perceived as pessimistic, just delete it. Focus on the happiest parts of your life and the things in life that truly make you HAPPY. Once a guy gets to know you (in the real world), then you can start revealing those other parts of your personality that might not be as "happy go lucky."

2. **Your Pictures Matter...BIG TIME:** Of course they do, this is what will pique his attention in the first place, so make them stand out. Get a few professional pictures taken if need be or at least run them through Instagram to get the right lighting. Also, a quick tip about online dating pictures — sometimes the pictures YOU think are most attractive are not the most attractive to guys. Be sure to rotate them and try different pictures each week until you find one that's getting the right type of attention from the right types of guys.

3. **Don't Be Afraid to Initiate:** Sure, it takes a little time and energy to send two to three messages per day, but consistency is key. Spend a little bit of time every evening messaging your top choices and see where it goes. *For example messages you can send guys to really get their attention, visit: www.sexyconfidence.com/secret/online/.*

Now, even though you're going to be spending a little time online, it does NOT mean that it replaces any of your time spent meeting guys offline. Online dating is simply a TOOL to help you meet people offline. Nothing more, nothing less. It's just a supplement to your offline socializing.

And the best part of online dating is these days you can actually tell people that you met online — it's 100% socially acceptable.

And if they try to make fun of you for meeting your boyfriend online, look them in the eyes, and yell, "Don't be such a Laggard!"

MINDSET 5

A Sexy Confident Woman Isn't Afraid of Being Considered a Little Weird

The other night I was talking to a girl I just met and I said something weird that just came to my mind. I told her, "There's nothing I like to do more than twerk on the dance floor." As I told her this, I busted out the illest, nastiest twerk anyone has ever seen.

Then after my insta-twerk (Insta-twerk: verb, to quickly proceed with the twerking movement after little or no warning), she looks at me and says something like: "OK, dude, you're kind of weird."

But since it was in my home town of Boston, it was probably more like: "You're a wicked EFFING weird dude. Get outta here, sucka!"

It was the ultimate twerkiller: (Twerkiller: To make someone feel like a weirdo for performing the insta-twerk).

I was officially a weirdo.

Now anytime we do something socially abnormal, our initial reaction is to conform back to the "norm" by retracting our weird comments, habits, or in my case, my dance.

But I didn't, I decided to follow the advice that I would give to any of my clients, and that is, to own my weirdness.

If you do something awkward or weird, just own it.

As my dad always says, "It's better to have people calling you weird, than to not be talked about at all."

And the best thing about being a little weird sometimes is that it can actually be an attractive quality.

It's a differentiator. And we all know that Sexy Confidence is about differentiation.

There's nothing worse than just being average, or "normal." Ugh.

I've discovered that most people who avoid being weird end up being what I call an indifferent personality. This type of person never seems to elicit any emotional response from others. People are just indifferent toward them.

Because even though that girl didn't like me, I still managed to elicit an emotional response. (Negative emotion is still an emotion!)

And if there's one thing I've learned from working with thousands of people on dating and relationships — it is that we're all total weirdos. And those who make fun of you for being weird are probably going home doing weirder stuff than you do.

And that's the beauty of being human. We all come from different backgrounds and have different experiences that are always going to weird out some people. But if you're not willing to share them, it's going to be impossible to create lasting impressions with the people you meet.

So embrace your weirdness and just accept that some people will be turned off by it. But it's worth turning a few people off when you finally meet someone you connect with who is wildly turned on by it.

Get out there and weird out a few guys. ☺

MINDSET 6

A Sexy Confident Woman Isn't Ashamed of Wanting Commitment from a Man

So you've met a guy and you've being seeing each other for a few months. But you're thinking to yourself, damn I want to lock this guy down for something a bit more serious.

And you want this guy to be your boyfriend so bad because he's just "perfect," but he doesn't seem like he wants to take this to the next level.

He only wants to see you during the week and just for sex. You haven't met any of his friends or family, and he doesn't show any depth of emotion to you…but in your eyes, "he's perfect."

Well, for starters, he's not the clearly not the perfect guy if he doesn't give you what you need.

So many women forget that a man's current relationship values are core criteria for defining the "perfect guy."

If he doesn't want a relationship and you do, then he's not "perfect" for you. Quite the contrary.

There's nothing wrong with a guy not wanting a serious relationship as long as he's upfront about it. Just the same with women — there's nothing wrong with you not being in a place in your life to find a committed relationship. That's OK, nothing to feel guilty about so long as you're not leading someone on.

But if you're seeing a guy who's clearly not looking for anything serious, but you're in a phase in your life where you are, then he is NOT perfect. His current relationship values are not in line with yours.

So when you're faced with this situation, you have two choices. Either give in to his demands, keep sleeping with him, then call him a "male pig" to your girlfriends when you learn that he's also seeing another woman.

OR, you can also be honest with him (and with yourself). After you've been seeing a guy for at least month or two, it's totally acceptable to simply explain to him that it's important for you to spend time with someone who values being in relationship. Assure him that you're not trying to put pressure on him, but you cannot keep seeing him casually. Then finalize the conversation that for now, maybe it's best that you just be friends.

After this conversation with you, a man will go home, sit down, and have a very REAL conversation with himself.

The devil inside of him will say, "Keep getting out there, having fun and see if you can do better."

The angel inside of him will say, "Just commit to her. She's so cool, and fun, and clearly she's girlfriend material because she stood up for herself and isn't willing to settle for a casual relationship that she doesn't want."

Then after that internal conversation, he'll make his decision. And because you showed this inner strength to openly confront him with this decision, your value as a woman to him will rise exponentially.

A Sexy Confident, high value woman isn't afraid to lose a guy if he's not giving her what she needs.

And no matter what he decides, you win.

If he wants the relationship, then great — you can now move forward with your life with him.

If not, you can now move on with your life without him — and spend your emotional energy finding someone who is ready for something more serious.

Sexy Confidence Success Story

"Adam, I used your example conversation script as a basis for a conversation with a guy I was seeing casually. By the end of our conversation, he was literally begging me to be his girlfriend. I wish I had met you ten years ago — but am so happy I know you now."

-Emily, 38 NYC

Download the script at www.sexyconfidence.com/discount80

MINDSET 7

A Sexy Confident Woman Will REJECT Mr. WRONG Even If She's Wildly Attracted to Him

A ttraction is a crazy emotion. And unfortunately, you cannot choose who you are attracted to.

Attraction is not a logical choice. *It's a feeling.*

The only thing you can choose is who you date. Who you date and wind up in a relationship with is always a choice.

So I've put together a list of the three different types of men that I've found women are HIGHLY attracted to (based on my experience of also being a dating coach for men). But here's the catch. The reason you're attracted to this type of guy IS the very reason why he's wrong for you.

The Challenging Chad

From the moment you met him, he'd be interested then uninterested, he'd be hot and then cold. He'll tell you he's never felt this way about a girl before, but then doesn't text you. You just don't get him.

And that's why you're so attracted to him.

We as humans value people or things that we work hard for. Unfortunately, when it comes to dating, usually the people we are most attracted to aren't that into us. And that's why we're so attracted to them!

But if you're looking for a happy fulfilling relationship, you'll realize you don't want to be with someone who is a challenge to win over. Instead just to be with someone who challenges you intellectually, who challenges you to be a better person, and who makes you a better person when you're around them.

Stimulation Seeking Stan

This is the guy who always wants the next best thing. He probably loves adrenaline sports, he's probably super competitive — he just loves stimulation. Stimulation Stan just hates sitting still.

He probably loves to go out a lot, loves to party — loves to do anything that gets him moving.

And that's why you like him. He's exciting. He's impulsive and each day is a new adventure. He's probably super passionate about whatever he's doing.

But if you're looking for some real relationship security, Stimulation Stan might not be your best bet. He's the dude to have a vacation weekend fling with…not to bet your future on.

The Guy Who's Always Surrounded by All the Girls...Gary

Back when I was coaching men on how to approach you, I would teach them how to be the guy who's always surrounded by all the girls...Gary. Why? Because women are psychologically more attracted to men who are surrounded by other attractive girls, rather than a guy sitting in a dark corner with a bunch of other dudes (AKA Creepy Cory).

This concept is known as *social proof.*

Basically, what this means is that if you see a guy at a party talking to an attractive girl, or a group of attractive women, then you will automatically assume there's a reason why they're interested in him. Even if he's not that physically attractive, you'll assume that he must be really funny, smart, wealthy, cool, or the owner of the bar...or something. You'll automatically give that dude more time of day than you would a guy sitting by himself in the corner (Creepy Cory doesn't get many dates).

But in general, you might want to think twice about only going for the guys who are always around other girls because...

They're always around a lot of girls!

And that likely means they may not be the most relationship-focused guys out there.

MINDSET 8

A Sexy Confident Woman Doesn't Overanalyze Whether or Not A Guy Likes Her

So let's start with the six most popular "signs" that a guy likes you.

1. He'll approach you and continue conversation with you.

2. He'll touch you or he'll break the touch barrier.

3. He's got positive upbeat body language — smiling, laughing and trying to make you laugh.

4. He's looking at you or even staring at you.

5. He compliments you.

6. He's playfully teasing or sarcastically teasing you.

But here is the biggest problem with all of this — a guy is only going to display these signs if he's experienced with women, or straight up, if the dude's got game.

But let me tell you something about men, most of us are not smooth. Most of us don't know what we're doing out there, and when we really like a girl, we sometimes do the opposite of these six signs I just mentioned.

I'm convinced that there are millions of potential couples out there right now, who both like each other but neither of them are sure of it and they don't end up together because no one's willing to make a move.

Such a shame.

So let's start with a basic three-step system to figuring out whether or not he REALLY likes you.

For starters:

#1: Does He Treat You Differently Than He Treats Other Women?

Maybe he teases you way too much or maybe he compliments you way too much. Regardless, he treats you differently than other women in his life.

#2: Take the gut check quiz

Most women seriously overanalyze whether or not a guy likes them — and the reality is that you probably know whether or not he likes you already. So I want you to imagine you're taking a multiple-choice quiz, and you have to choose yes or no to the following question: "Does he like me?" There's no maybe. There's no analyzing. You are graded on the correct answer. What would you choose? Chances are that your gut reaction is probably right.

#3: Show Some Interest in Him and See How He Responds

Next time you see him, give him a little indicator of interest by smiling, giving him a compliment and breaking the touch barrier when you compliment him.

See how he responds. If he's indifferent toward your advances, he's simply not interested. If he reciprocates flirtatiously, then let him start pursuing you.

It's really not rocket science, so stop spending all of your emotional resources analyzing a guy who isn't showing much interest in you.

Sexy Confident Women Are Happy When They Are Single AND When They Are In a Relationship. Their relationship status does not dictate the pleasure they receive out of life.

To learn the emotional attraction triggers, visit www.SexyConfidence.com/discount80

MINDSET 9

A Sexy Confident Woman Isn't Afraid to Tease or Disagree With a Guy She Likes

Recently, I went to a sixty-five-year-old married woman's dating seminar.

Her #1 piece of advice: "The goal of any conversation is to always be agreeable with anything a man says. Men want a YES woman."

Every woman in the room nodded incessantly as if this were profound advice.

I wanted to scream, I wanted to shout. I wanted to rip my hair out! OK, fine I really didn't care that much, but I was bothered by her advice.

But why, you ask?

Because men want to be challenged. We don't always want a YES girl. We want a YES/MAYBE/NO woman.

Sure, men want to date a woman with some similar interests, but we also want to date women with opinions that differ from our own. There's a critical balance to strike here.

Being overly agreeable is boring.

And being overly disagreeable is or "devil's advocate" breaks any hope for an emotional connection.

However, being teasingly disagreeable can be fun, flirtatious, and keeps a guy on his toes if done correctly.

For example, let's say a guy says, "There's nothing I'd rather do than ride my motorcycle every weekend." (FYI — this would probably be something I would say on a date).

Now if you absolutely LOVE motorcycles and would LOVE riding it every weekend, go ahead and agree. That's a cool commonality you share.

However, if you're like most non-leather chaps wearing females, you probably think motorcycles are loud, obnoxious and dangerous.

So rather than being overly agreeable and saying, "Yeah, motorcycles are cool," and faking your way through the date, or, alternatively, rather than straight up shooting him down and saying, "Motorcycles are for idiots, you know you can die right?" Teasingly debate him.

Maybe you could say, "Really? You don't do anything else on the weekends than ride a motorcycle? You actually kind of look like a motorcycle gang member."

He'll chuckle and reply, "Nope, that's ALL I DO on the weekends, and that's why I became a motorcycle gang member." Now, how much more flirtatious is that conversation?

Don't be afraid to give him shit sometimes, just do it with a smile.

Don't be afraid to push the envelope because confident guys don't like doormats. They want a woman who can challenge them and their BS.

Teasingly disagreeable can sometimes be more interesting than seeking commonalities.

And a lot of women forget that they are just as responsible for creating fun, light, exciting conversation as he is.

Let me give you a quick example of a client using this technique on a first date. Her name is Katherine, and she is a straight up city girl. She loves going out for nice dinners, she loves dressing well and shopping on the weekend. Now, she met a guy online, and according to her, "He's super buff," and seems super interesting.

The only problem?

According to her, "He's not a 'city boy.'" She exclaimed, "He's more of the 'camping outdoorsy type.'"

So she was asking me how she could learn more about hiking before her date so that she didn't look totally "dumb."

I asked her a simple question, "Are you legitimately interested in learning how to hike?"

She responded, "Not really. It sounds super lame."

Well then, just be teasingly disagreeable. When you talk about what you do for fun, be totally open with him about the fact that you are a city girl and you love going out for nice dinners.

He'll probably respond and tell you that he's more of "nature" type of guy than a city guy.

This is your moment to poke fun a little bit.

I explained, "Tell him 'So you spend your weekends hunting deer and wrestling bears? I'll stick with sushi dinners downtown,' and say it with the biggest smile on your face."

So she followed my advice.

As counterintuitive as it was, she told me that the moment she delivered that line, the entire dynamic of the conversation changed and he started to tease her back. She told me that was the moment some chemistry sparked, even though they were totally disagreeing with one another!

At the end of the night, they agreed the next time they saw each other, he would try sushi so long as she'd come with him to check out a new hiking trail up north. And what do yah know? They're now dating AND are stretching their comfort zones a bit.

All because she was willing to take a risk, be playful and tease him a little bit.

Don't be the boring agreeable date, challenge him and be amazed when you see him working for your approval.

Sexy Confidence Success Story:

"I'm recently out of a four year relationship and literally forgot how to flirt with men. Then I purchased your course online and learned how to unleash my own personality on a date without coming off as too brash. This has paid off ENORMOUSLY. Guys are getting to know the real me — and they are loving it! I have you to thank — so here's my official thank you."

Alexandra, 25 Wisconsin

Start this same journey by visiting www.SexyConfidence.com/discount80

MINDSET 10

A Sexy Confident Woman Realizes That Physical Beauty is Only ONE Part of Attraction

I believe that constantly trying to improving your looks is just like adding too much fertilizer when trying to grow flowers.

Let me explain.

I'm not a flower guy, and never will be. I like mud, I like "manly" things, and I don't spend my time growing girly flowers.

But the roof deck in my building had a flowerpot open, and I thought, "What the heck, I'll grow me some flowers."

So I asked my mom how I could have the most glorious flowerpot in the building. (Because we all know gardening is about WINNING, duh!)

She said, "Adam, you definitely want to start by getting some good fertilizer."

So I went to the local store, bought the most expensive fertilizer in the store and added it to my plants. And what happened? My flowers were looking about the same as the other flowers. So, I went back and spent more money buying more fertilizer thinking this would produce more results.

But after a while, my flowers started to turn brown.

And then finally, my flowers all died because I basically suffocated them with fertilizer.

Now, not only did I spend more money than anyone else on my flowers, but they ended up worse than everyone else's anyway.

So what'd I do wrong? What I didn't realize was a very important life principle, and that is the law of diminishing returns. This principle states that adding more of one factor, while holding all other factors constant, will at some point yield lower returns.

With my flowers, I didn't realize that fertilizer is only ONE critical factor of many, but because I focused so much energy on that one factor, I was forgetting about watering it properly, or the sunlight it was getting to grow.

So what the heck does this have to do with your physical looks when attracting men?

Well, it's simple. There are diminishing returns when it comes to your physical appearance and attracting men.

Unfortunately, most women think it's the only factor and put so much emphasis on their looks, that just like with the fertilizer, they ignore the other factors while suffocating themselves with makeup, unhealthy diets, and overly aggressive outfits thinking that's what really matters.

Sure that might get more men to want to sleep with you, but if you want relationship-focused men, personality will win every time.

So the answer to the original question is, yes looks do matter and it's important to try to look your best whenever you go out, but eventually it'll provide a diminishing return.

So here are the critical three steps I'd like you to take moving forward.

1. Focus more of your energy on improving how you convey your personality. Do you laugh every night you go out? Do you smile as much as possible? Are you a social risk taker? Are you teasing men as much as possible? Are you playful? Do you tell adventurous stories? Are you truly passionate about your life? Your personality is more improvable than you can ever imagine. It just takes energy and focus.

2. Ignore the physical attributes you can't improve: Maybe it's your facial structure, maybe you can't improve your skin condition or maybe you have a scar that isn't going away. Just realize there's nothing you can truly do about it and focus on what you can truly control. If it's something outside of your control, don't waste another iota of emotional energy trying to improve it. It's a lost cause.

3. **Address the physical aspects of your beauty that you actually can improve.** If you want to lose weight, stay on a new diet (I recommend the Paleo Diet or at the very least cutting out all grains from your diet). If you want to try new makeup, use it sparingly, but put it on any time you go out to meet new people. If you need a new haircut, put some thought into your cut and your hair stylist. If you want to buy the new red dress because you heard it's the most attractive color (which is scientifically true), then YES — do it. Just so long as you realize it will eventually provide diminishing returns.

And the most important part of all of this is that if you feel confident about your look, it will shine through in every interaction.

Because sure, some guys do only care about your looks — but those are generally the guys who are not looking for a relationship.

The "boyfriend material" guys are judging you based on your personality, vibe and character because those are the staples of a great girlfriend.

MINDSET 11

A Sexy Confident Woman Isn't Afraid to Initiate Conversation with a Man

You walk into a party and there's a hot guy there who's clearly working the room, and just like a wrecking ball broken lose from crane smashing you in the chest, you are knocked off your feet. He's sexy, he's cool, he's confident — but he's not looking at you.

What does a gal do?

This principle will teach you exactly how to approach him, without him knowing that he's actually being approached. If you get this wrong, you'll look desperate. Get this right, and you'll have the choice of any guy in the room.

By most women's standards, I'm categorically insane.

And this is mostly because I've approached literally thousands of women in my life and have tried almost every conversation starter on this planet.

And throughout my experiences coaching men on how to meet YOU, I've discovered that a guy cannot successfully approach a woman without the following three parts of the equation.

• A man must be engaging, funny, and different to successfully pique your interest.

• A man must be fully committed and bold so he doesn't look insecure.

• A man's body language must be casual so he doesn't look desperate.

Approaching women can be difficult for a guy.

But luckily for you, approaching a guy as a woman ONLY includes the last point of that equation?

You must be casual and seem as if it was just "fate" that brought you two together.

Now, unfortunately most women get this wrong. They assume the same principles of what works on them is equally effective when they are approaching guys.

Wrong!

You absolutely, positively 100% can approach men. However, it's only to serve one purpose: to give him an opportunity to win you over.

You don't need to be bold. You don't need to be funny. You just need to give him that opportunity to take the lead.

And this is why women approaching men is WAY easier than a man approaching a woman.

Just spend your nights going out and giving guys "windows of opportunity."

Have ever seen Jerry McGuire, when he says, "Help me help you."

All you're doing is helping him to help you by giving him an opportunity.

Here are a few examples of how you can casually approach a guy by giving him an open opportunity to talk to you.

• He's sitting at a bar watching the game, you ask him, "What's the score of the game?"

• He's in front of you at Starbucks, you ask him, "What do you think, is it too hot outside for hot coffee?" or "What do you think is it too cold outside for iced coffee?"

• You're at a lounge bar next to a guy about to order drinks, and ask him, "What are you drinking? I can't decide between beer or wine."

And when you deliver any of these you're smiling from ear to ear, are loving your night and are on the brink of laughter in every interaction.

Now, what do all of these conversation starters have in common?

• You said something and gave him a window of opportunity

• You said *something*...**ANYTHING**. You did it. And what did you give him? A window of opportunity!

• They were casual and not being too direct. (Too direct would be saying something like, "Hi I think you're hot and wanted to say hi." Barf.)

From now on I want you to take advantage of those short moments that occur throughout your life on a daily basis when you see an attractive guy and give him that chance to win you over.

It's time you realize that most guys are far too nervous to approach you. So if you're willing to take that first itsy bitsy step forward to give him that opportunity, you'll be amazed at how many guys will then take the second step to progress the conversation forward.

And if he doesn't, then chances are, he's not interested and that's totally OK. Because now you know how to meet other guys.

Sexy Confidence Success Story:

"I seriously cannot believe I did this — but I was dedicated to following your advice, and it paid off BIGTIME! I went out with my girlfriends last weekend and saw the hottest guy — I kid you not — I've ever seen. Normally, I would've just let it go, but I was dedicated to achieving the social score you set for me in the program, and asked him, 'Excuse me, do you know any good places around here where my girlfriends and I can go dance?' He smiled, told me where to go — and then asked me for my phone number so he could join later. He texted me later that night and met up with me — and we kissed. Now we've gone on five dates and he's already mentioned being my boyfriend a couple of times. I'd be 100% single for life if it weren't for you, Adam LoDolce. Thank you!"

-Allison, 34 San Francisco

I'll teach you more about how to initiate with men at SexyConfidence.com/discount80

MINDSET 12

A Sexy Confident Woman Puts in Effort Every Single Day to Overcome Her Shyness

Do you get really nervous around guys you like? Do you absolutely dread going to social events? Maybe you're a little shy, or you're just lacking a little confidence. Regardless, what if I were to tell you that starting today, you can be the most outgoing woman in a room?

Believe it.

These four tips will enable you to drop your shy mentality and allow you to be the life of the party starting today.

First, realize that No One gives a crap about you! You heard me, no one gives a crap about you, and I mean that in the most positive way imaginable. We as humans are so narcissistic that we when we walk into a room, we think that everyone's watching us because we are the center of our own universe. But in reality, everyone is in the center of their own universe, so if you do something stupid or embarrassing, just remember, no one's really paying attention!

Second, if you want to start being really social in a room, just focus on the goal of actually initiating lots of conversations, rather than the outcome of the interactions. This is called being Outcome independent. Stop concerning yourself with the outcome of an interaction and just be happy that you committed to making it happen. Set a goal to talk to five people in a given night and don't worry about ANYTHING else other than that behavior of just being social.

Third, when you walk into a room for the first time, don't forget to warm up. It's just like "stretching out" before a big workout. You see, I'm a big CrossFitter as you probably know, but what you might not know is that out of a one-hour CrossFit class, usually the workouts are only five to twelve minutes long. The rest of the time is focused on warming up and stretching. The same thing applies when you go out and meet guys. Spend most of your night just chatting it up with people who don't intimidate you, and then when the time is right and you're feeling "on fire," work your way closer to the guy across the room who you've had your eye on.

Finally, try committing to the "five minute rule." This means that you'll give ANYONE, and I mean, ANY freaking guy five minutes of your time. The only obvious exception is of course if you feel unsafe. Then please listen to your gut and leave the interaction.

I've noticed that most women spend their entire night fixating on one or two guys and wonder why they get nervous when they actually meet them. Open up your horizon to anyone in the room. It'll build your confidence and you just never know who might surprise you with some attractive banter.

Remember, shyness with men is something you can overcome. It just takes a little focus and a little action.

MINDSET 13

A Sexy Confident Woman is a Healthy Woman Who Goes to Healthy Places to Seek Healthy Men

Are you sick of meeting burger king eating, fried chicken loving smokers who drink too much on the first date? Well, I've discovered that most of the women who are a part of the Sexy Confidence Community are incredibly health-conscious women, and they want to meet guys with the same value system.

So here are five great places to meet health conscious men.

First off, join a running club. Here in Boston and in cities all across the country there are groups of people who get together, run and then grab appetizers afterwards. Some are more serious than others, so try a few different ones in your own city to find the right blend of socializing and exercising. Google "Running Club [YOUR CITY]" and sign up for one.

Not only are you going to get into better shape, but you'll have an opportunity to meet some great guys through the process.

Next, ditch yoga for a few days a week and join a CrossFit gym or some type of martial arts studio. I get it, I'm just another CrossFit cultist who won't stop talking about the "CrossFit Community," but if you're looking to meet quality health conscious guys, there are very few better places to go. Martial arts studios will also have a very similar type of guys. I had a client who started taking MMA classes, and met her boyfriend by kicking him in the face. (Not a bad story for the grand kids!)

Third, go to your local Adult Education organization for healthy cooking classes. Although the male/female ratio may not be as good as CrossFit, the guys who are there are definitely health focused. And the best part? If you end up dating, that guy's going to know how to cook you a mean breakfast in bed. You can thank me when you're eating your eggs with a delicious side of salmon and avocado.

Fourth, Meetup.com has a TON of activities clubs. Bust out the laptop and type in www.MeetUp.com to check out all of the FREE outdoor activities groups: Hiking clubs, rock-climbing groups, bike-riding groups too. You name it, you'll find a niche group that'll serve the purpose of keeping healthy while meeting health-conscious guys. And let me tell yah, the beautiful part about meetup.com is that so many guys are single and looking for you — yes you — you sexy little hiker you.

Lastly, join a coed intramural sports league. For example, here in Boston we have a sports league called Social Boston Sports where you can sign up to join sports leagues like softball, kickball or basketball. Many of the groups are coed and it's an amazing way to meet super active guys. There are leagues like this in cities all across the country. Trust me, I've looked them up for clients of mine, so they do exist in your given city. Simply google "Intramural Sports League in [YOUR CITY]."

So there it is, a list of all of these great places to go. And you're probably thinking to yourself, yah, that Adam guy is so right, I should do that. Then you'll go on with your day and then go to the bar again this weekend and never actually change any of your behavior. So instead of being part of the 95% of women who take no real tangible action, choose one activity that I mentioned here and sign up for it, right now.

Why isn't your lap top out?

Do it, now. :-)

MINDSET 14

A Sexy Confident Woman Holds A Smile Even When She Feels Like Frowning

Smiling is one of the most instinctive things we do. Babies smile, blind people who have never seen smile — the devil himself, I'm sure, smiles. But, when you see a guy you like, suddenly a toddler has an advantage over you in getting his attention. This principle will teach you the simple *do*s and *don't*s of getting a guy's attention with a smile so you don't look desperate or needy.

Imagine two guys are approaching you. Guy #1 is attractive and Guy #2 is a little less attractive. But Guy #1 has a Derek Zoolander expression while Guy #2 busts out the most radiant smile you've ever seen.

Who are you more interested in?

Pearly white guy will win every time. This is because a smile is the key to an unbelievable first impression. Just like you're attracted to a guy smiling, us men feel exactly the same way. So here's how to do it.

The Giggle Effect: If you make eye contact with a guy and want him to approach. Simply giggle to yourself and then look away. Avoid staring like a stalker, the giggle/look away effect gives him the hint without taking away the pursuit that he so desires.

The Lingering Smile: When you're walking around a room, hold a smile the entire time. It feels unnatural at first, but when I'm coaching my male clients out at night, I will literally giggle to myself as I walk around the room. No one knows you're giggling, they just think you're having an amazing night. Also, it's way easier to smile at someone if you're already smiling, than it is to pop a smile once you've locked eye contact.

Learn How to Smalk: When you're talking to a guy you like, practice the art of smalking: which is smiling while talking. Spend one minute in front of a mirror talking to yourself while maintaining a smile. You'll be amazed at the difference.

Comedy Forces a Smile: If you're just walking around — at a whole foods, on the streets, while shopping — try listening to standup by downloading the Pandora Apps and listening to a standup comedian (Daniel Tosh or Louis CK are two of my favorites). I assure you that you'll be giggling non-stop and attracting a lot of male attention.

Now, the law of attraction states that like attracts like. If you want to attract a fun, engaging and happy guy into your life, it's time you put a little focus on yourself to give that radiant vibe out there to the world.

MINDSET 15

A Sexy Confident Woman Surrounds Herself with Other Sexy Confident Women

I f you're single right now, finding few incredible wing girls is critical to successfully meeting great men.

Go to single events and meet the girls! Places like speed dating, singles mixers, meetup.com are, of course, packed with singles. If the guys are lame, chat up the girls.

You heard me. Hit on girls. Make Wing-Girlfriends.

You're at a networking event? The guys are hideous? Go mack on some ladies.

When you initially start wing girl hunting, don't be picky about what she looks like, instead look for women who have a positive vibe and energy. She doesn't have to be your BFF, your BFL, or your Friencess (friend-princess?), but she should make you FEEL great about yourself and be fun to go out with. This way when you're meeting men, you're not sitting in the corner miserable with a Debbie downer friend. Instead, because she's fun, you'll be portraying playful body language that will automatically attract more men to approach to you.

And remember, the most ideal man-hunting group is the crew of two, maybe the party of three — tops. And, definitely no boys allowed as your wingman, even if the guy is totally in your "friend zone."

No guys are going to approach you, and my sneaking suspicion is that if a dude is going out with you to "wing you," he's probably trying to hook up with you.

So flap those sexy wings and go find yourself a sexy confident lady or two to have some fun with.

MINDSET 16

A Sexy Confident Woman Understands that Sex ≠ Emotional Connection

Here's a question from one of my YouTube fans, Amy: "I've been hooking up with this guy for the past month and I get the feeling that it's all physical and no emotional connection with him. The worst part is, I'm starting to develop feelings for him but I'm scared to let my guard down, how do I know whether or not he feels the same way?"

Ah, so he wants the sex, but he doesn't want to make it complex? So frustrating.

The harsh reality is, though, men can have sex with a woman with literally ZERO emotional connection.

But it does make sense. According to many evolutionary psychologists, men are designed to spread their "seed" with as many women as possible to have as many offspring as possible. While women have very limited resources. Sex means more to you, because historically, AKA pre-condoms, it MEANT more to you, AKA getting pregnant.

So if you're looking for more than a just hookup, you're probably trying to figure out whether or not a guy is just trying to have sex or if he's also feeling emotionally connected.

Now here are basic signs he's emotionally connected (AKA likes you more than just in the sack).

He'll introduce you to his friends: A guy will never introduce a girl to his friends or family without having some future potential in mind.

He's willing to hang out with you during the day. If you're only seeing him when he's drunk or at the late hours of night, chances are he's only interested in sex.

He'll talk on the phone for extended periods. If he's talking to you over the phone, he's interested in your personality. He enjoys it and wants more of it. This is a clear sign of emotional attraction.

He'll do something more on a second/third date than just "go out for drinks." Men will invest their time, money and resources into you if they FEEL something for you.

Basically, you'll know he's emotionally attracted to you if he is generally willing to hang out without sex always being at the forefront of the activity.

Beyond those things, there's one thing women need to remember: Actions speak louder than words. What he DOES means so much more than what he says.

If you'd like to learn the seven ways to trigger a man's emotional attraction, head on over to www.sexyconfidence.com/discount80.

MINDSET 17

A Sexy Confident Woman Dates Just like a Single Man Dates

Most women will say that men are total disasters at dating. However, women can still learn a lot by emulating some of the things us men actually do get right.

For starters, men will gladly date multiple women until they are in a committed relationship. Never commit to a guy unless he has explicitly DTR'd you (defined the relationship). If you've been seeing each other for a while, and he hasn't defined the relationship, then simply ask him, "Should I be dating other people?" He'll be forced to say yes or no — without you having to ask him, "Are we in a relationship?"

Next, most men will talk to any woman for at least five minutes — we don't discriminate when it comes to socializing and flirting. As I mentioned a previous principle, we'll "warm up" and talk to a handful of women before even approaching women we're really interested in.

Stop writing a guy off completely or pushing him away because his first impression isn't the strongest. I've discovered that men are generally just much friendlier when they are out at night. It's so critical to make socializing a habit. At www.sexyconfidence.com/discount80 I'll teach you how to set the right type of "social goals" to meet more men.

Finally, men don't deal with wingmen who are being downers. If our buddy is being a Negative Nancy when we're going out at night, we'll leave him behind or call him out. Regardless, men don't accept that negative vibe because we know that it's going to hurt our chances out there. So why should you be willing to hang with your Debbie Downer every night you go out? We are products of the people we surround ourselves with, and if you keep going out with a girl who kills the group vibe, kindly tell her what she's doing or leave her at home.

Yup, you heard me. Leave her at home. She's not worth you being single.

MINDSET 18

A Sexy Confident Woman Will Break Up With Mr. WRONG

Here's a question from a YouTube fan, Jessica: "Adam, I love all of your tips and I've been meeting sooo many more men now, all thanks to you. But I have a bit of an issue now, I seem to be attracting the worst types guys. The last guy I dated cheated on me, and I'm concerned I'll just bring another bad guy into my life. Do you have any suggestions on how to filter for the wrong guys versus the right guys?"

Here's my response.

First off, you don't ATTRACT the wrong guys, you CHOOSE the wrong guys, so now it's a matter of figuring out how to pick the right types of guys.

Here are three things you should look for early in the relationship:

1. Look into His Relationship History: As my history teacher, Mr. Lachepelle, would say, "History repeats itself." By the second date you should know when his last girlfriend was and how long the relationship lasted. If he has never really had a girlfriend before, he's probably not a guy you want to invest much emotional energy into.

2. Be Mindful of His Lying Habits: If he lies about little things, he's probably lying about big things. I'm not counting white lies, such as him telling you that your meatballs are delicious.

I'm talking about weird little lies that are super sketchy.

You: "What'd you do last night?"

Him: "Nothing"

You: "Really? You check in on four squared at Hooters at 1:30 this morning."

To learn the six triggers that cause men to cheat, head on over to www.sexyconfidence.com/discount80.

3. Regularly Check in With How He Makes You Feel: Does he make you happy? Does he make you a better person? If he's putting you down now, it's only going to get worse. If he's bringing you down, he's only going to drag you through the mud.

And what's the hardest part about filtering out the bad guys? Actually filtering them!

Breaking things off is hard, but if the relationship is off, well then it's wrong. GET OUT. Filtering means that you actually make a decision to leave because you have enough self-respect and foresight to know that you can find a guy who isn't a super sketch ball.

It is better that you be lonely now than to be married and lonely later.

MINDSET 19

A Sexy Confident Woman Is Highly Social Because She's Learned to LOVE Socializing, Not Because She's "Man Hunting"

In December of 2013, I went on an unbelievable month-long trip to Thailand with my best friend from elementary school, Rob. We had the time of our lives exploring and backpacking all over the country.

Well, I guess I didn't really backpack. I was that guy who used the roller luggage.

Whatever, irrelevant, I was "backpacking."

Anyway, there were a ton of people in their twenties and thirties from all over the world backpacking either alone or in small groups. It was truly THE most social environment I've ever been a part of. And the women who were traveling there were seriously the most fun, social and friendly women I've ever met.

They were extremely positive about their own lives, and they asked me questions about my passions and interests.

And by the way, very rarely did they ask the most boring question most women will default to at a bar: "What do you do for a living?"

Instead they focused on more interesting aspects of who I am.

There was just a lot of genuine curiosity and interest and not questions because they were trying to categorize me into "boyfriend material." They were questions so they could really understand me as a person.

They were stress free, and the interaction was stress free — no pressure for it to BE something. The point of the conversation instead was all about being present and enjoying one another's company.

The conversations seemed to be the exact opposite of a typical single bar conversation.

And because of this stress-free environment, a true love story was created...

When I was on this small island called Kho Tao, we met a Swedish guy, an Australian, and a group of five Norwegian girls.

The Swedish guy, Freddy, met one of the Norwegian girls, Pia, and it was love at first sight.

And I mean it. He said to me five minutes later, "I'm going to marry this girl."

Then he changed all of his travel plans from that point on and moved to Norway to be with her.

UPDATE: Five months later they visited me in Boston on their way to South America for a six month travel excursion. They were the same lovebirds I had met months before in Thailand.

And I believe their relationship was formed because there was no pressure in the environment.

You don't have to be in Thailand to be super social and carefree. Try doing the following:

Walk around your city as if you've never lived there before. Ask people for directions (even if you know where you're going).

Be curious and friendly to everyone around you.

Be an explorer.

When you go out at night, go out as if you're on vacation. We all know that mentality. That fun-loving carefree "I don't care" mentality everyone has when entering a new city.

I know it can be tough to change your mentality when you've been living in the same place for so many years, but give it a shot and be a social backpacker in your own town.

Or a social roller luggage-er.

MINDSET 20

A Sexy Confident Woman Commits Her Life to Ongoing Self-Improvement

L earning to change is really a skill in itself.

The real reason most of my clients fail to transform their love lives is because they are too stubborn or afraid to try new things or ideas.

The more adaptable you are, the quicker you will see results. It really is that simple.

And quite frankly, I've never coached anyone who didn't have to change a part of who they were to be successful in finding or keeping love.

Yes, when you're dating I want you "to be yourself," but I also want you to improve yourself each and every day.

Improvement requires change. Maybe you need to change:

How you talk to yourself: Are you negative, are you unforgiving, are you tough, are you critical, are you spiteful, hateful? Imagine if you could change that conversation to love, acceptance and openness toward yourself. How might that attract great people into your life? Drastically.

How you speak to others: Do you talk down to others, are you depressing, are you pretentious, overly shy, and are you always seeking validation? Imagine if you could change how you communicate with others by being genuinely inquisitive, caring, and positive. Imagine if you could start really listening to people instead of always trying to do the talking. How might that attract new guys into your life? It will.

Your expectations of men and love: Do you believe that if you're not married by thirty-two, you're a failure?

The types of guys you go for: Do you invest yourself emotionally in men who are totally emotionally unavailable? Imagine if you decided today to ONLY invest yourself into someone who's willing to invest emotionally into you?

If we get to the core of why I created Sexy Confidence in the first place, it was to help women feel great about themselves through the constant pursuit of change and improvement. I believe that it is our duty on this earth to continuously experiment with new thoughts, new ideas, new actions, new conversations, new types of people, new types of venues in order to continuously improve our own sense of self.

But it is impossible to help anyone change if they don't want it. Do you want to change? Do you REALLY want to improve?

I'd like you to think of the power of elasticity, so let's take an object that is very elastic: the rubber band.

It fits around anything. It's flexible. It's fun to play with. It's fun to shoot at people in the subway.

I want you to look at your behaviors like a rubber band. Don't be afraid to stretch out a little bit and just see what works for you.

Open up your mind to new experiences. Allow yourself to be vulnerable again, stretch your social comfort zone, say hello to someone you would've never talked to previously, wear a new outfit that might be a little radical, go to a singles event that makes you nervous, be a little overly sarcastic on your next date and see how he responds, confront the guy you're currently hooking up with that's only using you for sex and tell him that you're not that type of a girl. Constantly strive to improve through the act of change.

And if, for whatever reason, the rubber band breaks, you can simply tie the knot (heal your wound), and your weakest link now becomes a strength. For example, if you do let a guy into your life, and he breaks your heart, realize that this is a natural part of life. Learn and grow from the experience, and you will heal and become even stronger.

Today is the day to change because there will never be a better day, I assure you.

So how do you commit to making a change in your love life?

Find the Reason: First, you must answer the question of "Why." Why is this change important to you? Why do you want a relationship? Why is it important to go to every party you're invited to? Why should you start smiling more every time you go out? Answering the question of "Why" will keep you on track when you inevitably do hit a roadblock.

Baby Steps: Second, remember that it's OK to take baby steps. Start small because small steps produce the momentum for you to take larger steps. How do you eat an elephant? A bit at a time. If you haven't been on a date in six months, it would be overzealous to set a goal of going on six dates in the next month. Ease into it and don't overextend yourself too quickly.

Build Your Support System: Next, don't be ashamed to ask for support. We all need someone who believes in us and our ability to change and improve. If you have someone who supports you, tell them about the change you plan to make in your life. If you don't have that person in your life, start supporting other people unconditionally — and you'll find that others will want to support you in return.

Learn How to Change: You should find a mentor who has a track record of helping other people change in the same way you want to change. In your love life, I will continuously guide you through this process of change and improvement.

Set Your Expectations: You must realize that positive change doesn't always happen in an instant. Sometimes you will be taking one step backward, in order to take two steps forward. For example, let's say you've decided to break it off with a guy because he doesn't meet your new found standards. At first when you break it off with him you might be ridden with heartbreak, but in two months, you'll find that you've taken many new steps forward with your life.

So now it's time for you to commit to a critical change in your life.

Choose one critical aspect of who you are that you want to improve. If you can't decide which one to hone in on, brainstorm all of them on one sheet of paper, then find the one change that will have the greatest impact on happiness in your life. Remember, change takes focus, don't try to do too much at once.

This is what I want to change about my love life (be specific):

_____

_____

_____

Now, answer the question, "Why is this change important to me?"

_____

_____

_____

Next, find one tangible action you can take immediately, and I don't mean in a few hours, I mean, immediately. I'm going to put this book down right now and go do:

_____

_____

Then, call your support system and tell them about the change you're making in your life. Ask them for their unconditional support because of how much this change means to you.

Now for the fun part, which is figuring out the "how to" roadmap. My advanced thirty-day program will guide you through the majority of the changes that need to be made in your love life *(www.sexyconfidence.com/discount80).*

If the change is outside of your dating life, find a mentor who can help you such as a business coach or a personal trainer.

Finally, set your expectations and create a realistic timeframe on how to make this happen.

And in the words of an ancient Chinese philosopher, Lao Tzu, "If you do not change direction, you may end up where you are heading."

Success Story:

"Adam, your program is exactly what I needed to create long-lasting change in my love life. I always followed the same patterns with the same (wrong) guys — and now I'm in the happiest relationship of my life. Your program was literally priceless."

Rebecca, 43 Arkansas

MINDSET 21

A Sexy Confident Woman Spots and Avoids Crazy Men Like the Plague

I've admittedly dated a lot of women in my life, and at one point in my life, I just thought all WOMEN were crazy!

But then I started coaching women at SexyConfidence.com on how to meet quality men, and you know what I realized?

Guys are also fucking nuts. I heard some stories from women that literally blew my socks off.

So that basically affirmed that people from both genders are cray cray.

But since this book is designed for women, here's a list of signs that you're dating (or have dated a crazy guy):

Stalker Syndrome: He knows way more information about you than you've ever told him. For example, he knows exactly where you eat lunch in the park every day, but you've never told him anything about your lunch breaks…

Socially Unaware: He texts all of your friends, and he's not really friends with your friends yet.

The Needy Ned: He constantly shows up to your house unexpectedly just because he wants to "see" you (but really he's checking up on you).

The Social Media Maniac: He writes on your Facebook wall, and you don't write on his. He keeps poking you on Facebook, and you take seven weeks to poke him back. He likes all of your posts, and you do NOT like his posts.

The Hypocrite: He gets mad at you for having a password lock on your phone…and the reason you have a password lock on your phone is because you he is…insane.

He constantly asks about your past exes, but he is totally evasive about his past relationships

Unsafe Sex: He tells you that he wants to have unprotected sex with you even though you remind him constantly that you're not on birth control. Then you start to hear the sound of a baby crying…

The Accuser: He constantly makes false accusations. For example, "What took you so long to get home from the volunteer night at the food kitchen? Are you banging a homeless guy?"

The Guy Who Just Won't Go Away: He won't let you break up with him. I recently met an older married couple and asked them how they met. She said they met in college, and she kept trying to dump him but he wouldn't go away. Awkward!

The Needing a Challenge Chad: He tells you that he's head over heals in love with you, and the moment you tell him you feel the same way, he decides that he wants to be with someone else.

Taking It Way Too Far: When you two argue, he always seems to take it to a new level.

For example, you might say, "Listen I think you need to learn how to communicate a little better with me."

And he harshly responds, "Oh you want to hear me communicate? You're breath always smells like a baby's diaper and you're just not a funny person at all. You've never even really made me laugh! Oh and one other thing I hate your mother!" Yeah, that guy's bat shit crazy.

The Control Freak: He doesn't allow you to have any guy friends, and you've repeatedly told him that "Guyfriend" doesn't equal "Sexfriend," boyfriend or affair, it means FRIEND.

The Contradicting Cory: He constantly contradicts himself by telling you that he needs some space, but that he can't wait to snuggle later.

The Physical or Emotional Abuser: But most importantly, the biggest sign that he's crazy is if he either verbally or physically abuses you in any way, shape or form. Leave him right now. It will not get any better and he doesn't deserve you.

So if you're currently dating a crazy person and you like it, well maybe you're also a crazy person and you both can be crazy together. And if you don't like it, "woman up" and leave him. Life's too short to surround yourself with erratic, emotionally uncontrolled people.

MINDSET 22

A Sexy Confident Woman Realizes That When a Guy Disappears, It's HIS Loss. She simply says, "NEXT!"

Have you ever started seeing a guy, it's going well, you're starting to like him, great vibes, then suddenly the guy vanishes. It's as if he died, or turned into a ghost.

And unlike the 1990 hit movie Ghost with Patrick Swayze and Demi Moore, he doesn't come back from the dead to make clay pots with you.

Nah, sorry, you're making some clay pots on your own this time.

The dude is gone, and he's not coming back, and you're wondering what the heck happened.

Well here are five common reasons why men disappear so suddenly.

Some Men Are Terrified Of Break Ups: Men are cowards and we avoid confrontation like the plague. Think of it this way, it's a lot easier to start something with someone than to end it with someone. So more guys will just disappear than take the manly way out and end it like a gentleman.

He's a Player and Doesn't Want to Play You: If a guy is in a phase where he wants to date or sleep around, sometimes he'll disappear on a woman he's afraid of hurting because he senses you like him more than a "casual situation." So he "Peaces out" to avoid hurting your feelings. If this is the case and he disappeared, it's 100% for the better.

He Likes You, but Doesn't Love You: Dating is tough sometimes, and sometimes a man likes a woman, but then realizes shortly thereafter that he's just not in LOVE with that woman. Maybe he likes you a lot, but realizes there's no future potential so he moves on.

You haven't been dating long enough to warrant a breakup: If you've only gone out with a guy for one, two or even three dates, don't expect him to end it with you. Even if you slept with him, don't expect that he'll have the guts to straight up break it off, or that it's even the social normal for him to break it off. If you can't handle that, then don't sleep with him until he's showing more signs of relationship potential. Realistically, don't expect a true breakup unless the relationship has been clearly defined.

Maybe you're not listening to him: Maybe he's tried to make it clear that the relationship isn't going anywhere, but you wanted it to go somewhere so badly that you ignored him and kept trying to push it forward — texting him, trying to see him again, or sleeping with him casually. Then he realizes that his only way out is to POOF into thin air.

An external circumstance that has NOTHING to do with you: If you can't pinpoint WHY a guy has disappeared on you, then just assume something has come up in his life. Maybe he got back together with an ex, maybe he just got fired from his job, maybe he's moving — who knows. Don't agonize for weeks or months over this one guy. Just assume something came up, and it wasn't the right time in his life to be with you.

So moving forward, be sure not to put all of your eggs in one basket. Unless you're in a fully defined committed relationship, you should continue to socialize with and date other guys until it is monogamous on BOTH ends. This way, if a guy does decide to peace out on you, you'll have other options available to you.

Listen, I'm not going to pretend that there's an easy way around all of this, and dating can be really difficult and frustrating sometimes. But don't give up, and just realize, if a guy does disappear on you, it's ALWAYS his loss.

To learn the warning signs of a guy disappearing, start the advanced video training program at www.SexyConfidence.com/discount80

MINDSET 23

A Sexy Confident Woman Works Hard Every Day to Overcome Her Insecurities, While Realizing That Insecurity is Perfectly Natural

L et me tell you, I've had a rather rough few weeks of feeling a little insecure about myself.

Why?

Because for the vast majority of my last three weeks, I've had a cream caked on the side of my lips which is a mixture of Neosporin and anti-fungal cream.

Yes, I've had foot cream on my face for the past three weeks. Barf city.

You see, I have what is apparently known as angular cheilitis, which is a fungal condition where the sides of your lips get dry and crack open.

Nope, it's not herpes and it's not contagious. It's just this horrible fungus, gross cracked, red side of my lip that everyone sees the moment they look at me.

And it's not like I have a lot going on right now, and it's not like I'm throwing a big birthday party and inviting people over that I haven't seen in years or that I have speaking engagements in front of thousands of people. And no it's not that I've been kissing my lady.

And when I say no, I actually mean yes, I had to do all of that with my angular cheilitis.

So I wanted to talk about insecurities because I'm not going to lie, I've been pretty insecure about anyone looking at my face for the past few weeks.

Now, maybe you don't have angular cheilitis, but we ALL have an ITIS of some sort — basically something we don't like about ourselves that make us self-conscious.

Maybe you feel you're too overweight to be sexy, or you feel like you don't have much of a personality, or that you're too shy, or that you have a big nose, or small nose, or big hands, or little person hands, or are too tall, or you're bad in bed, or that men don't like you, or that girls don't like you, or that you don't know how to dress well, or that you dress too flashy, OR maybe you're just so insecure because you feel totally inadequate to be with someone else romantically.

Regardless of what types of insecurities you have, it's time to start addressing them immediately. Because when it comes to dating and relationships, men are generally less concerned about your actual "condition" — whatever it may be — and are MORE concerned with how secure or insecure you feel about it.

Step #1: Improve what you can, ignore what you cannot. If you have something about you that makes you feel insecure, ask yourself one question — is this something I can actively change about myself?

If this is something you cannot change, such as a permanent disability or a physical defect, then realize it is totally outside of your control and isn't worth your mental energy. Many times, self-acceptance is the critical component to self-esteem.

However, if this is something you can actively improve upon, then start taking some tangible action to improve whatever it is that's making you insecure. Even just the smallest of all improvements will immediately make you feel better about it. Confidence is built through systematic small steps that lead you to a big change.

For example, let's say you're too self-conscious to make any jokes or banter in a social setting. Sign up for a class on comedy — or read a book on comedy. Take some tangible action right now, today. Even just the act of doing something about it will make you feel better immediately.

Step #2: Fake It Till Yah Make It. Our brains are so wildly powerful that you can trick your brain into believing ANYTHING you tell it. Never underestimate the power of positive thought. Let's say you feel a little insecure about your weight and don't feel very sexy.

I'd like you to imagine how you'd act if you were in what you would consider to be, "perfect physical shape." How would you act, how would you talk, how would you think, how would you express yourself. What would you do differently? How would you interact with men?

Look yourself in the mirror and say this ten times out loud. "I have the sexiest body out of any woman in the room."

Now imagine that woman, and now simply pretend that you are that woman the moment you walk into a room. Fake it till you make it and trick your brain into believing it's true.

Your brain is painfully gullible, and sometimes all you need to do is stretch the truth so it believes you.

Step #3: Contradict Your Brain. Identify the real root causes of your insecurity, then find some evidence that totally contradicts it.

Let's say you're nervous about meeting new people. Well, get to the root cause of why you feel this way. I've found that most people, in this case, are afraid of rejection or embarrassment.

Then once you have that root cause, I want you to go back into your memory and think of a few times when you met someone new and had a fantastic conversation — and were NOT rejected or embarrassed. Visualize those moments any time you feel the insecurity creep back in again.

And above all, never forget to love yourself and every single imperfection you have.

Even if it's angular cheilitis.

Because no one is perfect and if you can't love yourself, it's going to be nearly impossible for someone else to do that for you.

MINDSET 24

A Sexy Confident Woman Doesn't Invest More in a Man Than He Invests in Her

Dating can be tough, and the worst scenario that can happen is when we like someone, and it's starting to become pretty clear that the person doesn't really like us.

But what do we do when that happens?

We deny it.

And we waste all of our energy and resources on that person.

When we really should be saying one word: "Next!"

Here are the six signs that a guy just isn't into you so you can begin moving on with your dating life a little bit and invest your energy into a guy that IS investing himself into you.

Sign #1: He treats you like a friend or like one of the guys. Women can definitely be friendzoned just as often as men are. And if a guy is into you, he's not going to treat you like one of the guys.

Sign #2: You're constantly pursuing him: Generally, when a guy is into a woman, he's going to want to keep talking to that woman and seeing her again (the only exception to this rule is if he's extremely shy and only about 10% of men fall into this category). So if he's not trying to progress things forward, he's probably just not that into you. Stop pursuing him and stop trying to spend so much time with him. See what he does. If he starts putting in more effort, then GREAT! If not, it's just not meant to be. NEXT!

Sign #3: He's a Painfully Slow Texter: Listen, this is not a steadfast rule, some guys just aren't good texters, myself included. But if he's not wanting to communicate with you regularly, chances are he's blowing you off. When a guy is really into a girl, he cannot help but wanting to be in touch with her.

Sign #4: He's only available to hook up or have sex on weekend nights past the hour of 1 a.m. If you receive the following text:

"He Jensyf, watu doin rihgt nowe? Want ot hag out?"

Have the self-respect to not respond (unless of course you're only interested in a casual quicky). If he does like you more than just a quicky, he'll text you the next morning embarrassed about what he did and wanting to make it up to you. Then of course, use your best judgment if you're willing to LET him make it up to you.

Sign #5: He openly talks to you about other women he's attracted to. If he says something like, "Hey jenny, I matched with this woman on OKcupid and I'm definitely in love. This is the one I've been looking for my whole life." He's probably not really that into you. Sure, maaaybe he's trying to make you jealous, but in all reality, if a guy is really attracted to a woman, he's not going to risk it by trying to make her jealous.

Sign #6: He's always busy. A guy will make time for a woman he's interested in. I have a super busy schedule, but when I'm dating someone I'm totally smitten for, she comes first above all else. And you know what, if he's not willing to give you his time, just realize that you deserve to be with someone who will and move on. There is a guy out there who will make the time for you.

Now I know this section might not be the happiest part of the book for everyone reading it. Maybe you've realized that a guy you're totally into, might not feel the same way toward you.

And if that's the case, ask yourself one important question.

"Who the F cares?"

One critical component to dating is being with someone who wholeheartedly wants to be with you and who will treat you the way you deserve to be treated.

If that's not happening now, you're better off knowing it now rather than wasting six months with a guy only to realize he wasn't that into you.

Lift your head up and realize there is someone out there who wants to be with you, who appreciates you for who you are, and who won't let anything stop him from being with you.

To learn some key strategies on how to get a man to invest more in you on an emotional level, simply visit www.SexyConfidence.com/discount80.

MINDSET 25

A Sexy Confident Woman Isn't Afraid to Be a Polarizing Personality

The other night I was out with a group of friends, and there was a woman from New York who wouldn't stop talking about "how awesome Manhattan is." She kept saying, "It's betta than every other city out there — way betta than boring Boston."

Now for starters, I love Manhattan, and I even lived there for a short period, but I hate annoying people who think their city is better than everyone else's.

So of course, I had to respond, "Yeah Manhatten's fun, but only when you're not there thinking your city is better than everyone else's. I bet it's actually a lot of fun right now."

(Silence falls upon the room).

Now was I trying to be a jerk? Not necessarily, but I spoke the truth and I totally won over the other 90% of people having to listen to her who were thinking the same thing (trust me, by the expressions on everyone else's faces, they were relieved when I called her out).

Something I've learned over the years of dating coaching is that confident people aren't afraid to be hated sometimes (this woman definitely disliked me after this comment).

Controversy is a natural part of conversation and confident people aren't afraid of expressing their opinions...even if they're going to be disliked by some people.

I personally follow what I call the 90/10 rule, which means in order to get 90% of people to really like you, you're going to generally have 10% of people dislike you, or even hate you sometimes. And that is perfectly OK.

And don't be nervous to be controversial with people when you first meet them. Studies have shown that within three seconds to fifteen minutes of meeting you, people are drawing one of three conclusions.

They either like you, don't like you, or are totally indifferent toward you.

Now as a dating coach, you would think I would work with a lot of "hated people" who need to be nicer in general to people.

Quite the contrary.

When I first started coaching everyone, I noticed very shortly that everyone was very pleasant.

Almost too pleasant.

Sometimes even to the point of being unauthentic.

And that's because many of my clients are classic "people pleasers." They do anything in their power to make sure EVERYONE likes them, because they are terrified of anyone NOT liking them. So they always put everyone else's thoughts, opinions and needs ahead of their own.

And by doing so, they are actually achieving a different result than getting people to like them. Generally, people just seem to feel indifferent toward them. No one feels very strongly either way about them. I call them an "indifferent personality."

AKA a "meh" personality.

And in my opinion, this is the absolute worst of all personalities to have. I'd rather be wildly hated than for people to have no opinion about me.

We all have strong opinions — and if you don't have strong opinions, form some. Become educated on topics, get out a little — and then speak your mind. Some guys will hate it, some guys will love it — but at least you're injecting some emotion into the conversation.

So begin living by the following two principles.

If you disagree with someone, go ahead and disagree with them. Sometimes you can connect with someone on a deeper level through disagreement than you will through mindless agreement (refer back to the teasingly disagreeable section).

Stand up for yourself: If someone is manipulating you, call them out on it. Don't be a doormat and be willing to confront someone when necessary without constantly fearing reprisal.

Realize that being controversial can be a very attractive quality to the RIGHT person. Strong statements can elicit either very strong positive responses or negative responses (hence why it is polarizing).

So get out there. Go ahead, find a few haters, and stop trying to please everyone because it's not possible.

Oh, and if you're discovering that way more than 10-20% of people hate you, then you're probably just a bitch — and perhaps it's time to be a little nicer to people. ☺

MINDSET 26

A Sexy Confident Woman Speaks Openly, But Still Knows How to Maintain a Healthy Filter around Men

L isten, we all say things we know we shouldn't have said.

I've been there. Recently I told a woman that I do naked sit-ups in the mirror every morning.

Talk about a gross mental image.

So in this section, I've compiled a list of things women have actually said to me when I was dating them or when I was on a date with them, and almost all men would agree that these should have been filtered from communication.

"I've lost track of the number of guys I've slept with, but I know it's a lot." Listen, I'm all for women's rights to be sexually promiscuous, but I'm not for ANYONE's right to advertise it. And that's true whether you're a man or a woman. This is the ultimate turn off. So if your number is up there, keep it to yourself, guys don't want to know about it.

"I honestly hate men, and I definitely don't need a man in my life." There are a lot of men out there, including myself, who deeply desire an independent, strong woman and I don't believe that a woman needs a man to be happy. But with that said, Men want to feel needed and appreciated in a relationship. If not, they'll just go somewhere else where they are needed, and of course, wanted.

"So I know we just met, but are you looking for a relationship?" To that I would say, "Yes, you're right, we just met, and to answer your question, no, not with you!" A first date is NEVER the time to ask if a guy is looking for a relationship, and quite frankly, you shouldn't even CARE if he is or isn't when you're on a first date. Focus on your energy on getting to know each other better first, then cross that "relationship" bridge if and when you both think there's chemistry.

"I feel fat, Adam, do I look fat?" Men love women who love their bodies and I know that's not always possible, but just don't ask guys about this. We're dating you because we're attracted to your body. And on top of that, it's not like a guy is ever going to say, "YES, you look fat." So don't ask a guy, save your breath.

"My Dad never likes the guys I date." And then I'll just be thinking to myself, "Then he probably won't like me, and hopefully he's not a member of the NRA." I get it, we all have crazy families, but try to make a man feel confident when he finally meets the parents — assure him that there's no reason they wouldn't like you. Even if you're telling a bit of a white lie.

"I don't care what any girls say, size definitely matters." There's only ONE circumstance when you can say this, and that is if you're dating a male porn star. Otherwise, keep your size opinions to yourself because if he's insecure about sleeping with you, size really won't matter because he won't be able to perform anyway.

"I always seem to date jerks." And he'll be thinking, "Does that mean I'm a jerk?"

"Guys always seem to disappear after a few months of dating me." And to this he'll be thinking, "Well since we've only been dating for a month or so I cannot wait to see what's in store for this next month!" Sometimes it's best to hold back a little information about your past negative dating experiences so you don't scare off a guy you've only just met.

"Ugh, you remind me of my ex." And he'll just simply respond with, "Oh, cool, what's his number? Maybe he and I can go hang out instead!" No one wants to be compared to an ex. He's an ex for a reason, and guys know this is NEVER a compliment.

So there it is, nine things NOT to say to a guy. Before you say something along these lines, think about how it'll make HIM feel. Empathy is critical to long-term dating success.

And if you do end up saying something to a guy that you totally regret, just remember, we've all been there.

There really are no mistakes or failures in life, only lessons.

So learn from them, keep growing and have some fun.

Oh, and if you do naked sit-ups in the morning...don't talk about those either.

Success Story:

"Adam, I grew up in a female dominated household and never really understood how to interact with men until I started to date. Needless to say, I wasn't very good at it. It took me twelve years to realize I needed help — and that's when I found you. Your advice has helped me tremendously and I can't thank you enough. I've never felt more confident around men."

Casey, 31 West Texas

Become the next Sexy Confidence success story:

www.SexyConfidence.com/discount80

MINDSET 27

A Sexy Confident Woman Is Empathetic Toward Men, Rather Than Constantly Blaming Them for Wrongdoing

D ating is difficult for women.
I mean, you can't outwardly "pursue men," if you sleep with men too quickly they'll judge you, and if you wait too long they'll think you're a prude.

But you know what? Dating isn't just difficult for women, it's challenging for EVERYONE (men included).

So based on my coaching so many men over the years on how to meet and flirt with you, I thought I'd share with you five secrets that most women don't really know about men.

#1: We are absolutely terrified of approaching you.

When a guy hires me to teach him how to approach women, he literally doesn't sleep for five days before our session together. I meet him, he has bags under the eyes, and he's shaking like a leaf — because he knows he has to face his fear of meeting women. And that's the effect you have on men when we're attracted to you.

So please, cut us a break if we're a little awkward when we first approach you. And you know what? It's really your fault for being so damn sexy.

#2: We're emotionally closed off, not because we're jerks but because we're terrified of what these emotions might actually mean.

Emotions are terrifying for us. For our entire lives, men have been taught to be tough, not to show emotion or be vulnerable. And when we feel weak with emotion, we try to toughen up — out of habit. I mean, do you ever see guys talk out their emotions with one another?

If you're finding we're closed off to you emotionally, you need to understand that our feelings may be so intensely strong for you that we really don't know what to do with them.

#3: Ultimately, we really do want love, but our strategy and timing to find love might be a little different than yours.

Maybe our path involves sleeping with fifty women to get an idea of what it is we really want, both physically and emotionally.

But even if we're doing that, we're probably still looking for love...eventually. We're just going about it a little bit differently than you. Whereas your strategy might involve staying miles away from any man who's slept with fifty women.

Timing is really key here, though — and maybe you want love sooner than he wants love. You can't blame him for that, and you can't blame yourself. It's just a mismatch. You aren't meant to be.

You will meet the right person at the right TIME in both of your lives — and if it doesn't match up, it's not meant to be.

#4: Men really don't understand that women don't fully understand men.

We assume that women always get our signals — however subtle they may be — and so long as we're throwing out the signals, we're off the hook for any wrongdoing.

Let's say a guy is only calling you on the weekends at 2 a.m. Most men assume that the woman will "get the hint that it's only about sex." Unfortunately, when you really like a guy, you end up missing the message he's "trying" to send you.

If he's throwing out mixed signals then it's your responsibility to set your boundaries with him about what's acceptable and what's NOT acceptable.

And if he's not following those boundaries, it's time to move on. Communication is key here, and sometimes you need to be the bigger person and have that conversation with him if he's falling out of line.

#5: When a man really likes (or loves) a woman, any guy, even a player can turn into a total clinger.

There isn't a man on this planet — I don't care how big of a lady's man he is — who hasn't fallen way too hard or way too fast for a woman and acted like a "Needy Ned."

If a guy is being a little overly clingy with you, don't immediately label him insecure. Maybe there's just something about you that he so deeply desires and it's causing him to go a little overboard to gain your attention.

MINDSET 28

A Sexy Confident Woman Is Social and Friendly with Everyone, Even Strangers (In Safe Environments of Course)

Ever since we were children, we were told never to talk to strangers, and this was for very good reason at that age.

But unfortunately, EVERYTHING we learn at a young age resonates with us for a lifetime.

Now before the internet came along, when we became adults, we had to unlearn this childhood principle very quickly. Because if we didn't, our social lives would be pretttty limited. You'd have to spend your nights reading Romeo and Juliet to get even a taste of romance.

Back then, there was no choice but to be social and talk to people you didn't really know. You'd have to get out there, in real life, and meet real strangers, or be alone wallowing in your sadness.

But today it's much different. We have iPhones, Facebook, forums, Twitter, Tinder that make us feel as if we're connected. But really they're only making us feel slightly satiated.

Then to compound it, we hear stories on the news of people getting killed, or murdered, or raped, and rightfully so, our reaction is to retreat further into our shell out of fear of strangers.

And you know what's happened to the world?

We've become unfriendly.

We've lost our sense of community.

Maybe you think its wishful thinking, but I still believe a man should go talk to a woman he finds attractive in the park.

Maybe you think it's crazy for me to say a woman should smile at a guy at the coffee shop.

But let me tell you something, none of this is really that crazy.

So long as you're in a safe, public area with plenty of other people around, friendliness is a key component to living a fruitful social life.

Anytime I, or any of my male clients, talk to a woman in the park, who is a stranger, generally she finds it refreshing and says, "Wow, no one ever does this anymore."

And as a man, when a woman smiles at us in the grocery store, we think to ourselves, "Wow, no one ever does this anymore."

I believe it is our responsibility as members of society to talk to strangers...

...in order to learn and grow from a new random perspectives.

...in order to have a few awkward moments and realize that awkwardness can be funny sometimes.

...in order to embarrass ourselves every once in a while so that we can learn to be more comfortable with who we are.

...in order stop living our lives with an irrational fear of all strangers.

Because yes, there are bad people out there, but the vast majority of us are harmless.

Most of the time when you talk to strangers, interactions will be short and quick, but sometimes, they will be surprisingly meaningful.

Even more meaningful sometimes than the interactions we have with our friends, family or coworkers.

So today is the day to talk to someone you've never met before.

Go ahead, smile at someone you don't know.

Say hello to a guy or gal walking by.

Compliment a guy on his jacket or shirt.

Genuinely commit to asking someone, "How is your day so far?" rather than saying it passively.

Go ahead and ask for directions instead of using Google Maps.

Take responsibility for creating a sense of community around you.

MINDSET 29

A Sexy Confident Woman REFUSES To Settle for An Emotionally or Physically Abusive Relationship

I'm totally perplexed that any man would ever lay a hand on a woman or even dream of it. I believe if you truly love someone, you could never intentionally harm them.

I've discovered there are two types, and only two types, of men on this planet: men who hit women, and men who wouldn't dream of it. And if any man ever lays a hand on you, unfortunately he falls in the first category, and he's going to do it again. So take action today — immediately remove yourself from the relationship. This clear line must be drawn.

Now, as you may have realized in your own life, not all abuse is physical.

Emotional abuse can be just as bad if not worse than physical abuse. A bruised lip can hurt you for months, but a bruised mind can hurt you for a lifetime. And because I know love can create blinders that don't allow you to see the storm you're trying to navigate, I've compiled the top seven signs you're in an emotionally abusive relationship.

#1 He's a psycho sadist. He literally feels better about himself the more than he puts you down. Maybe he constantly humiliates you, criticizes you, or embarrasses you. But as a sexy, confident woman, any of these are unacceptable. A guy in a healthy relationship will be a "super supportist."

He props you up when you're in need — and you do the same for him because it's a healthy relationship.

#2 He Always Comes First. You're forced to always put his needs in front of your own because you're scared of how he might react. A healthy relationship means you put him ahead of yourself because he's always putting your needs in front of his own — thus creating symmetry. If the relationship is too one-sided, it will fail. When it does, don't stay there to pick up the pieces. Just walk away in search of the right type of balance and chemistry.

#3 You Are Always the Problem. He makes you believe you are the reason the relationship is struggling — or that you're the crazy one. You're the one who needs to change and you're the one who needs to put in the effort, not him. Alternatively, a healthy relationship is — not to be overly cheesy —all about teamwork. If something is off, you put your heads together to figure it out together. If it can be solved, great! You solve it together. If it can't be solved, it ends.

#4 He cheats on you or intentionally tries to make you jealous. A healthy relationship is one without lies, deception or manipulation, and if you've committed yourself wholeheartedly to him, it is 100% expected that he do the same for you. And if he's not holding up that end of the bargain, it's your turn to make him crazy jealous when you break up with him and finally find a great guy who treats you with respect and love.

#5 He treats you like a pet, not like a person. Does he control where you go and what you do? Does he keep you from seeing friends or family, or limit your access to money, the phone or the car? Constantly check up on you? A healthy relationship is an equal relationship. If he's trying to be your owner, bite his hand off. No, just kidding, don't bite his hand off, just break up with him.

#6 Everyone's always better than you. He makes you feel inferior by negatively comparing you to other people or other women. Does he always prey on your greatest insecurities? If he's doing this, communicate how it makes you feel, maybe he doesn't realize what he's putting you through. But if it continues, perhaps it's time to rethink the relationship and move on to a man who supports you wholeheartedly.

A healthy relationship might still involve comparisons, but only in the positive sense of it. For example, "You are such a better girlfriend than any of my friends' girlfriends. Thank you for being great." Now that's a comparison you should enjoy.

#7 You're afraid of him. The antonym (or the opposite) of "afraid" is confident. If there is fear in a relationship, it's impossible for you to feel confident in your actions or words. So end it. And if you're too afraid to end it, it's time to get help. Try the hotline to gain more guidance: http://www.thehotline.org/.

Remember, being single is ALWAYS better than being abused, regardless of whether it's physical or emotional. You don't need a man's permission to do anything in life. Today is the day to stop always being the giver without receiving anything.

Give yourself permission to walk away from a toxic relationship.

Give yourself permission to walk away from any man who hurts you.

Give yourself permission to find happiness

Because if a relationship doesn't make you a better person, it's the wrong one.

And when you do move on, don't be afraid to open yourself up again. Don't let one bad experience make you hardened to life. Don't let his pain make you hateful. Don't forget that this world is still full of incredible love, and it is your G-D given right to discover it and embrace it.

If you find yourself in a physically or emotionally abusive relationship and need help, please visit www.TheHotline.Org.

Adam LoDolce

MINDSET 30

A Sexy Confident Woman Only Invests Energy into a Guy Who She'd Consider "Boyfriend Material"

Are you sick of bringing home the bad boy to your parents?

Or are you tired of meeting guys who might seem great on paper but bore the living shit out of you?

Well you're in luck. I've devised a simple two-factor checklist for you to consult any time you're analyzing a man's future potential.

Factor #1: Chemistry. Do you have a good conversational flow? Is the guy funny, does he excite you, do you have great sexual chemistry? Are you comfortable just being YOU around him. Chemistry is something I think we can all agree either exists or doesn't. You can usually determine that pretty quickly when you meet a guy.

Factor #2: Long-term Compatibility. Now this is a bit trickier to figure out. Do you share the same values — religious, family values, life philosophies? Do you both like spending your time doing the same types of things? Does he have a job? Do you both want kids (or not want kids)? The list goes on.

It's impossible for a guy to truly be boyfriend material unless he meets both of these standards. If a guy only meets one of these factors, it's going to be a disaster. Here's why.

Scenario #1

Let's say you meet a guy who you have great chemistry with. He's fun, he's exciting, and he makes you laugh. But reality sets in and you realize he has no job, he has radically different religious views than you, he lives three hours away and he never plans on moving out of his parents' house. Maybe you can have a short-term vacation fling with him, but if you decide to stay with him, soon enough there are going to be some major issues. It's a simple equation:

High Chemistry + Low Compatibility = Volatility

It might be a passionate relationship, but it's going to be full of arguments and fighting soon.

Scenario #2:

Now let's look at the opposite side of the spectrum. Have you ever dated a guy who is great on paper? He has a great job, he also loves hiking, he has a 401K, he's in the same church or temple as you, but he's just lame and super boring. You try to make it work because, dang it, he meets everything you think you want in a man. But you realize after a few months that you can't force yourself to have chemistry with him.

You realize that attraction is not a choice. You can't CHOOSE to be attracted to man, regardless of how hard you try. It's a simple equation:

Low Chemistry + High Compatibility = You Cheating (or strong desire to cheat)

So now you know. When you're dating a guy, don't lose focus on both of these two factors and don't settle if one of them is missing. And if you discover that one of them is missing, you have two choices.

Choice number one is to spend the rest of the relationship saying the following three words, "PLEASE, JUST CHANGE!"

OR, choice number two is to realize that you can't expect someone to change for you and dump the dude to find someone who meets both criteria.

I personally believe that choice number two is always the way to go.

MINDSET 31

A Sexy Confident Woman Doesn't Overcomplicate What It Is That Men Want

I'm about to answer a something that most women think is as complicated as: "What's the meaning of life?" or "Why do men have nipples?"

Well let me tell you, the answer to the question, "What do men really want in a woman?" is far simpler than either of those questions.

I've managed to boil this down to the core of what men really want in a woman. Here are the six key components that we're looking for.

#1: We want a woman who makes US feel like a man. These days strong, independent women are crushing it in the work place and establishing total dominance over their male counterparts and I think that's great. But unfortunately, some women take this same mentality of dominance and bring it into a relationship. They then wonder why the only men who stick around are wussy beta males.

Just like a magnet, a confident, dominant man is going to be attracted to a woman who complements his manliness with her femininity.

This doesn't mean the relationship isn't equal, quite the contrary actually. If you're attracted to a dominant/take charge man, you need to allow him to be that man by having the courage to step back and let him lead. I believe it takes more courage for a woman to let a man be dominant than it does for her to try and always take charge of the situation (which is a total attraction killer for most men).

#2: We want a woman to be fun and playful. I'll be the first to admit — who a person marries is probably the most important and serious decision they will ever make in their entire life. But, when you're with a guy and actually dating, you can't think of it that way.

Live in the moment and just enjoy the moment. Laugh with him and sometimes laugh AT him. Don't be afraid to poke fun of his quirks and, if he teases you, lightly punch him in the arm with a smile. (Lightly — remember, femininity!)

If you constantly put too much pressure on a man to be in a serious, committed relationship, he's going to cave under that pressure. He'll run toward his freedom (or toward a woman who's a little less serious and just more fun).

Enjoy your time together, and after a few dates of really goofing with one another, you can transition into more serious conversations.

#3: We want a woman who passionately loves her own life.

No man wants a life with you unless you have an incredible life without him.

If you're miserable now, a relationship will not necessarily make it better. Work on yourself first. Discover some passion in your own life first and when you do, men will take notice of it and want to be a part of it.

#4: We want a woman who we're physically attracted to, but who is also physically attracted to herself.

Regardless of what you look like, there are guys out there who are wildly physically attracted to you. Every guy has different tastes in women, and I assure you there's a man out there who has a taste for you. That sounds really naughty…but it's true.

But the thing that's more important than men being physically attracted to you is YOU being attracted to YOU. Take care of your health and your body. Put time into thinking about what you wear, not because you want to win over a certain man, but because you want to feel great about who you are.

When you think you look ugly, well, you're going to look ugly.

And when you think you look sexy, well, let me tell you — there's nothing sexier.

#5: We want a woman who is honest and trustworthy.

Don't lie to a man because you're afraid of what he'll think about the truth. Don't be sketchy because you're unsure about what you want. Being open and honest requires vulnerability, and even though that can be scary sometimes, you need to do it. It's impossible to truly connect with someone if that connection is based on lies.

#6: We want a woman who knows how to communicate her needs.

I think everyone can agree, communication is really complicated and difficult when it comes to such an emotional thing as dating.

If you feel like he's manipulating you, sit him down, face your fears and tell him what's on your mind.

If you think he's lying to you, don't engage in passive aggressive behavior, just sit him down and tell him about your suspicions (assuming they are within reason).

"Adam, the male mind has always been a mystery to me, until I found your program. You always seem to know exactly how to break down something that 'seemed' complex into something so simple. It's helped me in all aspects of my life — beyond just dating and relationships. Thank you — you have a fan for life."

Patricia, 43 Boston

To learn what men really want in a relationship, start your free video training at www.sexyconfidence.com/discount80

Adam LoDolce

MINDSET 32

A Sexy Confident Woman Doesn't Follow Old-fashioned Dating Advice

I'm sure your grandmother is a sweet woman, but she probably doesn't know the first thing about dating these days.

I've found there are four critical pieces of dating advice that are generally pretty useless for most people. I'm going to rephrase them to actually be of use to you.

#1: "Just Get Out There."

Oh really, maybe a woman should just walk down an ally in New York City and look for a man? Or maybe she could stand on the side of the street, lift her skirt a little bit, throw out the thumb and meet a good guy?

Instead of "Just get out there," it should instead be more like "Figure out what you LOVE to do, and go do those things in a social setting where there are men."

I guess it doesn't have the same ring to it.

Start making socializing a regular part of your life, and not because you're going "man hunting" but because want to do it and you ENJOY doing it. Because if you're not having fun in a social setting, you're not going to attract any great guys anyway. Men go for women who have a great vibe to them, and if you're not enjoying yourself, they're going to avoid you like sandals in a snowstorm.

Check out meetup.com or Eventbrite.com to find some new and interesting events in your area. Tough Mudders, CrossFit, coed sports leagues, Adult Education courses, and painting classes are all great ways to "get out there" by doing something you LOVE doing.

#2: "Just be yourself."

About six years ago I learned to play the guitar and like most people I wasn't very good. I tried to learn it on my own, but I finally I gave in and hired a guitar teacher. When I sat down with him, he listened to me play for a moment and then said, "You know what, Adam? You should just play what you want to play and people are going to want to listen." I thought to myself, "Thanks, dick." But he was right, I sounded terrible because I wasn't actually practicing the RIGHT way.

Instead of "just be yourself," it should be "Continuously focus on self-improvement, be open to trying new things, and when you meet someone, be your best most passionate, charismatic, and interesting self."

Socializing and dating are learnable skills, just like playing the guitar.

You can't just play any guitar chord you want and assume people are going to want to listen.

And you can't be just this unfiltered, miserable person and expect someone is going to want to date you.

#3: "Play Hard to Get."

I'm only going to slightly change this one from "Play Hard to Get," to "BE Hard to Get." If a guy likes you, it should be hard for him to win you over, but not because you're playing games. Instead you should be hard to get because you have so many amazing things in your life that you're not going to hand it all over to a guy without him earning it.

Keep investing in your own growth by staying socially active, and this will help you actually be the challenge he so desires. When you fake it and play games, he'll sense it and lose interest. When you're a legitimately interesting person with an active lifestyle, he'll work hard to be a part of it.

#4: "You'll meet someone once you stop trying."

Perfect. So, women, you should basically stay home, watch reruns of *Friends*, and you know what…he'll find you. That was me being sarcastic.

This saying should actually be, "You'll discover a great relationship once you stop forcing it."

You should never stop trying to get out there and meet new people. And when you do finally find someone you click with, you won't have to force him to be with you because he'll be working hard to be with you. And if he doesn't, he's not meant for you.

About the Author

Author of two books on dating and confidence, Adam is considered by many of the top psychologists, therapists and life coaches as one of the top dating confidence experts in the world.

After touring the world and speaking at over one hundred of the country's top universities (including Notre Dame, University of Alabama, and University of Texas, etc.), he's refocused his efforts to address a burning need: helping women build the right type of confidence to be successful with men. He's been coaching, writing, and speaking on dating dynamics for over four years now. He's also an MTV MADE coach and has been featured in thousands of the top media outlets such as *Glamour, Cosmo, Women's Health, The New Yorker* (and many more).

He has helped hundreds of self-proclaimed "helpless" women find love within weeks (not months) and has also coached some of the most powerful and successful women on this planet (foreign and national government officials, fashion experts, corporate executives, etc.).

He dedicates his time to CrossFit, yoga, golf, and traveling and is very close with his parents (Ann and Michael) and his brother (and best friend), Marc.

19273516R00087